Cycling
in
THE SOUTH WEST
OF IRELAND

Published by Collins
An imprint of HarperCollins*Publishers*
77–85 Fulham Palace Road
London W6 8JB

www.collins.co.uk
www.bartholomewmaps.com

First published 2002
Copyright © HarperCollins*Publishers* Ltd 2002
Maps © Bartholomew Ltd 2002

Collins® is a registered trade mark of
HarperCollins*Publishers* Limited

Routes compiled by the following:
Neil Wheadon.

Design by Creative Matters Design Consultancy, Glasgow.
Typeset by Bob Vickers.

Photographs reproduced by kind permission of the following:
Neil Wheadon.

The Publishers welcome comments from readers. Please address your letters to:
Collins Cycling Guides, HarperCollins Cartographic, HarperCollins Publishers,
Westerhill Road, Bishopbriggs, Glasgow, G64 2QT or email cycling@harpercollins.co.uk

Printed in Thailand

ISBN 0 00 712390 6
02/1/12

CONTENTS

KEY TO ROUTES

Route		Grade	Distance km (miles)	Time to allow	Page
1	Ballyheigue and Kerry Head	moderate	17.5 (11)	1–2 hours	14
2	Adare and Curraghchase Forest Park	moderate	19 (12)	2–3 hours	16
3	Lough Gur	moderate	20 (12.5)	2–4 hours	19
4	Ringaskiddy and Cork	easy	21 (13)	1–2 hours	22
5	Cork and Blarney Castle	moderate	22.5 (14)	2–3 hours	25
6	Rosscarbery and Glandore	strenuous	23 (14.5)	2–4 hours	28
7	Goleen and Mizen Head	moderate	25.5 (16)	2–3 hours	31
8	Skibbereen and Baltimore	moderate	26.5 (16.5)	2–3 hours	34
9	Kinsale	moderate	30.5 (19)	2–4 hours	38
10	Tralee, Fenit and Ardfert	easy	34.5 (21.5)	2–4 hours	42
11	Ballybunnion and Carrigafoyle Castle	easy	37.5 (23.5)	2–4 hours	46
12	Dunquin and the Dingle Peninsula	moderate	40 (25)	3–5 hours	50
13	Killorglin and Glencar	moderate	43.5 (27)	3–5 hours	54
14	Kilgarvan and Lough Atooreen	strenuous	45.5 (28.5)	5–7 hours	58
15	Castletown Bere and Allihies	strenuous	49 (30.5)	4–6 hours	62
16	Cahir and Clogheen	easy	53 (33)	4–6 hours	65
17	Tipperary and Galbally	moderate	53 (33)	4–6 hours	69
18	The Dingle Peninsula	moderate	59.5 (37)	5–7 hours	73
19	Killarney and Gap of Dunloe	strenuous	59.5 (37)	4–7 hours	77
20	Waterville and Valencia Island	strenuous	63.5 (39.5)	4–7 hours	80
21	Bandon and Clonakilty	moderate	77 (48)	5–8 hours	85
22	Glengarriff and the Beara Peninsula	strenuous	91 (56.5)	6–10 hours	90
23	Tralee and Dingle	strenuous	99 (61.5)	6–10 hours	95
24	A grande randonnée – the Ring of Kerry	strenuous	130 (81)	1–2 days	99
25	A grande randonnée – Mizen Head and Sheep's Head Peninsulas	moderate	131 (82)	1–2 days	104

Distances have been rounded up or down to the nearest 0.5km (mile).

undemanding rides compiled specifically with families in mind
16–32km (10–20 miles)

middle distance rides suitable for all cyclists
32–48km (20–30 miles)

half-day rides for the more experienced and adventurous cyclist
48–64km (30–40 miles)

challenging full-day rides
over 64km (over 40 miles)

grande randonnée – a grand cycling tour
over 100km (60 miles)

 Routes marked with this symbol are off-road or have off-road sections
(includes well-surfaced cycleways as well as rougher off-road tracks)

Black Valley, Killarney

LOCATION MAP

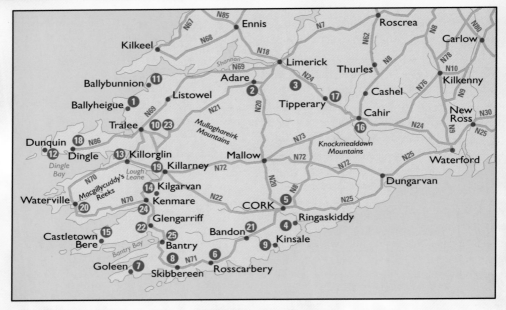

KEY TO ROUTE MAPS

M23 / Service area	Motorway		Cycle route / optional route	☎	Telephone
N18	National Route / Dual carriageway		Start of cycle route	开	Picnic site
R319	Regional road / Dual carriageway	12	Route direction	▲	Camping site
	Good minor road	B	Place of interest	♦♦	Public toilets
	Minor road		Public house	†	Place of worship
	Track / bridleway		Café / refreshments		Viewpoint
	Railway / station	✗	Restaurant		Golf course
	Canal / river / lough		Convenience store		Tumulus
	Ferry route	i	Tourist Office		Urban area
250	Contour (height in feet)	P	Parking		Woodland

Height above sea level

	250	500	1000	1500	2000	2500	3000	feet
	76	152	305	457	610	762	914	metres

INTRODUCTION

How to use this guide

Collins' *Cycling in the South West of Ireland* has been devised for those who want trips out on their bicycles along quiet roads and tracks, passing interesting places and convenient refreshment stops without having to devise their own routes. Each of the 25 routes in this book has been compiled and ridden by an experienced cyclist for cyclists of all abilities.

Cycling in the South West of Ireland is easy to use. Routes range from undemanding rides compiled specifically with families in mind to challenging full-day rides; the type of route is easily identified by colour coding (see page 5). At the start of each route an information box summarises: total distance (in kilometres/miles – distances have been rounded up or down throughout to the nearest 0.5km/mile and are approximate only); grade (easy, moderate or strenuous based on distance and difficulty); terrain; an average time to allow for the route; directions to the start of the route by car and, if appropriate, by train.

Each route is fully mapped and has concise, easy-to-follow directions. Comprehensive information on places of interest and convenient refreshment stops along each route are also given. Accumulated mileages within each route description give an indication of progress, while the profile diagram is a graphic representation of gradients along the route. These should be used as a guide only.

The following abbreviations are used in the route directions:

LHF	left hand fork
RHF	right hand fork
LHS	left hand side
RHS	right hand side
SO	straight on
SP	signpost
TJ	T junction
TL	turn left
TR	turn right
XR	crossroads

Cycling in the South West of Ireland

This guide contains routes through Cork and Kerry. Cork is Ireland's largest county. Cork city and environs, on the River Lee, are full of maritime history. Elsewhere, the county has a beautiful coastline of coves and peninsulas, cliffs and sandy beaches. The interior is generally rural – fertile farmland and lush green valleys. Kerry has dramatic mountains and moorland, cliffs and bays. Bordering the Atlantic Ocean, there are often magnificent far reaching views. Some areas of Kerry, such as the well-known Ring of Kerry, are particularly busy during the tourist season – the routes stick to quieter roads as far as possible, keeping cyclists away from the tourist buses. Both areas contain the remains of ancient civilisations, as well as modern visitor centres.

There are a few sections of off-road riding in this guide, but the majority of the routes follow quiet, almost empty minor roads through a predominantly rural landscape. Beware of encounters with farm dogs which will probably bark fiercely at bicycles. Also keep a lookout for sheep and cattle wandering on the road. Place names will often be spelt differently on signposts than on maps, and older signposts show distances in miles, while new ones indicate distances in kilometres.

Preparing for a cycling trip

Basic maintenance

A cycle ride is an immense pleasure, particularly on a warm sunny day. Nothing is better than coasting along a country lane gazing over the countryside. Unfortunately, not every cycling day is as perfect as this, and it is important to make sure that your bike is in good order and that you are taking the necessary clothing and supplies with you.

Before you go out on your bicycle check that everything is in order. Pump the tyres up if needed, and check that the brakes are working properly and that nothing is loose – the brakes are the only means of stopping quickly and safely. If there is a problem and you are not sure that you can fix it, take the bike to a cycle repair shop – they can often deal with small repairs very quickly.

When you go out cycling it is important to take either a puncture repair kit or a spare inner tube – it is often quicker to replace the inner

Café at Goleen

tube in the event of a puncture, though it may be a good idea to practise first. You also need a pump, and with a slow puncture the pump may be enough to get you home. To remove the tyre you need a set of tyre levers. Other basic tools are an Allen key and a spanner. Some wheels on modern bikes can be removed by quick release levers built into the bike. Take a lock for your bike and if you have to leave it at any time, leave it in public view and locked through the frame and front wheel to something secure.

What to wear and take with you

It is not necessary to buy specialised cycling clothes. If it is not warm enough to wear shorts wear trousers which are easy to move in but fairly close to the leg below the knee – leggings are ideal – as this stops the trousers catching the chain. If you haven't got narrow-legged trousers, bicycle clips will hold them in. Jeans are not a good idea as they are rather tight and difficult to cycle in, and if they get wet they take a long time to dry. If your shorts or trousers are thin you might get a bit sore from being too long on the saddle. This problem can be reduced by using a gel saddle, and by wearing thicker, or extra, pants. Once you are a committed cyclist you can buy cycling shorts; or undershorts which have a protective pad built in and which can be worn under anything. It is a good idea to wear several thin layers of clothes so that you can add or remove layers as necessary. A zip-fronted top gives easy temperature control. Make sure you have something warm and something waterproof.

If you wear shoes with a firm, flat sole you will be able to exert pressure on the pedals easily, and will have less work to do to make the bicycle move. Gloves not only keep your hands warm but protect them in the event that you come off, and cycling mittens which cushion your hands are not expensive. A helmet is not a legal requirement, but it will protect your head if you fall.

In general it is a good idea to wear bright clothing so that you can be easily seen by motorists, and this is particularly important when it is overcast or getting dark. If you might be out in the dark or twilight fit your bicycle with lights – by law your bicycle must have a reflector. You can also buy reflective bands for your ankles, or to wear over your shoulder and back, and these help motorists to see you.

You may be surprised how quickly you use up energy when cycling, and it is important to eat a carbohydrate meal before you set out. When planning a long ride, eat well the night before. You should eat small amounts of food regularly while you are cycling, or you may find that your energy suddenly disappears, particularly if there are hills or if the weather is cold. It is important to always carry something to eat with you – chocolate, bananas, biscuits – so that if you do start fading away you can restore yourself quickly. In warm weather you will sweat and use up fluid, and you always need to carry something to drink – water will do! Many bicycles have a fitment in which to put a water bottle, and if you don't have one a cycle shop should be able to fit one.

It is also a good idea to carry a small first aid kit. This should include elastoplasts or bandages, sunburn cream, and an anti-histamine in case you are stung by a passing insect.

It is a good idea to have a pannier to carry all these items. Some fit on the handlebars, some to the back of the seat and some onto a back rack. For a day's ride you probably won't need a lot of carrying capacity, but it is better to carry items in a pannier rather than in a rucksack on your back. Pack items that you are carrying carefully — loose items can be dangerous.

Getting to the start of the ride

If you are lucky you will be able to cycle to the start of the ride, but often transport is necessary. If you travel there by train, some sprinter services carry two bicycles without prior booking. Other services carry bicycles free in off-peak periods, but check the details with your local station. Alternatively, you could use your car – it may be possible to get a bike in the back of a hatchback if you take out the front wheel. There are inexpensive, easily fitted car racks which carry bicycles safely. Your local cycle store will be able to supply one to suit you.

Cycling on-road

Cycling on back roads is a delight with quiet lanes, interesting villages and good views. The cycle rides in this book are mainly on quiet roads but you sometimes cross busy roads and have stretches on A and B roads, and whatever sort of road you are on it is essential to ride safely. Always be aware of the possibility or existence of other traffic. Glance behind regularly, signal before you turn or change lane, and keep to the left. If there are motorists around, make sure that they have seen you before you cross their path. Cycling can be dangerous if you are competing for space with motor vehicles, many of which seem to have difficulty in seeing cyclists. When drivers are coming out of side roads, catch their eye before you ride in front of them.

You will find that many roads have potholes and uneven edges. They are much more difficult to spot when you are in a group because of the restricted view ahead, and therefore warnings

need to be given. It is a good idea to cycle about a metre out into the road, conditions permitting, so that you avoid the worst of the uneven surfaces and to give you room to move in to the left if you are closely overtaken by a motor vehicle.

Other things to be careful of are slippery roads, particularly where there is mud or fallen leaves. Sudden rain after a period of dry weather often makes the roads extremely slippery. Dogs, too, are a hazard because they often move unpredictably, and sometimes like to chase cyclists. If you are not happy, stop or go slowly until the problem has passed.

Pedalling

Many modern bikes have 18 or 21 gears with three rings at the front and six or seven on the back wheel, and for much of the time you will find that the middle gear at the front with the range of gears at the back will be fine. Use your gears to find one that is easy to pedal along in so that your feet move round easily and you do not put too much pressure on your knees. If you are new to the bike and the gears it is a good idea to practise changing the gears on a stretch of flat, quiet road so that when you need to change gears quickly you will be ready to do so.

Cycling in a group

When cycling in a group it is essential to do so in a disciplined manner for your own, and others', safety. Do not ride too close to the bicycle in front of you – keep about a bicycle's length between you so that you will have space to brake or stop. Always keep both hands on the handlebars, except when signalling, etc. It is alright to cycle two abreast on quiet roads, but if it is necessary to change from cycling two abreast to single file this is usually done by the outside rider falling in behind the nearside rider; always cycle in single file where there are double white lines, on busy roads, or on

Glandore

narrow and winding roads where you have a restricted view of the road ahead. Overtake on the right (outside) only; do not overtake on the inside.

It is important to pass information to other members of the group, for example:

car up – a vehicle is coming up behind the group and will be overtaking;

car down – a vehicle is coming towards the group;

single up – get into single file;

stopping – stopping, or

slowing/easy – slowing due to junction, etc., ahead;

on the left – there is an obstacle on the left, e.g. pedestrian, parked car;

pothole – pothole (and point towards it).

Accidents

In case of an accident, stay calm and, if needed, ring the emergency services on 999. It is a good idea to carry a basic first aid kit and perhaps also one of the commercial foil wraps to put around anyone who has an accident to keep them warm. If someone comes off their bicycle move them and the bike off the road if it is safe to do so. Get someone in the party to warn approaching traffic to slow down, and if necessary ring for an ambulance.

Cycling off-road

All the routes in this book take you along legal rights of way — bridleways, byways open to all traffic and roads used as public paths — it is illegal to cycle along footpaths. Generally the off-road sections of the routes will be easy if the weather and ground are dry. If the weather has been wet and the ground is muddy, it is not a good idea to cycle along bridleways unless you do not mind getting dirty and unless you have a mountain bike which will not get blocked up with mud. In dry weather any bicycle will be able to cover the bridleway sections, but you may need to dismount if the path is very uneven.

Off-road cycling is different to cycling on the road. The average speed is lower, you will use more energy, your riding style will be different and there is a different set of rules to obey — the off-road code:

1 Give way to horse riders and pedestrians, and use a bell or call out to warn someone of your presence.

2 Take your rubbish with you.

3 Do not light fires.

4 Close gates behind you.

5 Do not interfere with wildlife, plants or trees.

6 Use only tracks where you have a right of way, or where the landowner has given you permission to ride.

7 Avoid back wheel skids, which can start erosion gulleys and ruin the bridleway.

Some of the off-road rides take you some miles from shelter and civilisation — take waterproofs, plenty of food and drink and basic tools — especially spare inner tubes and tyre repair equipment. Tell someone where you are going and approximately when you are due back. You are more likely to tumble off your bike riding off-road, so you should consider wearing a helmet and mittens with padded palms.

Useful contacts

Cycling organisations
CTC — see page 111

Sustrans
www.sustrans.org.uk

Cycling websites
Online resources for cyclists in the UK
www.cyclecafe.com

Internet bicycling hub
www.cyclery.com

Information and support for cyclists in the UK
www.cycleweb.co.uk

Cycling information station
www.cycling.uk.com

Local cycle hire & cycle shops
Casey Cycles & Gas Supplies
New Street
Caherciveen
Telephone (066) 9151316

Cycle Repair Centre
6/7 Kyle Street
Cork
Telephone (021) 4276255

Cycle Scene
396 Blarney Street
Cork
Telephone (021) 4301183

Finnegans
37 Henry Street
Kenmare
Telephone (064) 61083

Fios Feasa Rent A Bike
Holyground
Dingle
Telephone (066) 9151606

Irish Cycling Safaris
Belfield House
U.C.D.
Dublin 4
Telephone (01) 2600749

Kirrary House Bicycle Hire
Avondale
Dingle
Telephone (066) 9151937

Jem Creations
Ladybird House
Glengarriff
Telephone (027) 63113

Paddys
Dykegate Street
Dingle
Telephone (066) 9152311

Rothar Cycles
2 Bandon Road
Barrack Street
Cork
Telephone (021) 4313133

Supervalu Supermarket
Castletownbere
Telephone (027) 70020

Tralee Gas & Bicycle Supplies
Strand Street
Tralee
Telephone (066) 7122018

Tourist information
Ireland's National Tourism Service
www.goireland.com

Irish Tourist Board
www.ireland.travel.ie

Tourism Ireland Ltd
Telephone 00 353 1 4182208

South West Regional Tourism
Telephone(021) 4255100
www.cork-kerry.travel.ie

Bantry Tourist Information Office
Telephone (027) 50229

Blarney Tourist Information Office
Telephone (021) 4381624

Caherciveen Tourist Information Office
Telephone (066) 9472589

Clonakilty Tourist Information Office
Telephone (023) 33226

Cork City Tourist Information Office
Telephone (021) 4273251

Dingle Tourist Information Office
Telephone (066) 9151188

Glengarriff Tourist Information Office
Telephone (027) 63084

Kenmare Tourist Information Office
Telephone (064) 41233

Killarney Tourist Information Office
Telephone (064) 31633

Kinsale Tourist Information Office
Telephone (021) 4772234

Macroom Tourist Information Office
Telephone (026) 43280

Midleton Tourist Information Office
Telephone (021) 4613702

Skibbereen Tourist Information Office
Telephone (028) 21766

Youghal Tourist Information Office
Telephone (024) 20170

Public transport information
CIE (Ireland's national transport company)
www.cie.ie
Telephone (09065) 500000

Weather forecasts
These two sites contain weather forecasts
for Ireland

http://interactive.iol.ie/today/weather

http://homepages.iol.ie

An Óige (Irish Youth Hostel Association)
Telephone (01) 8304555
www.irelandyha.org

BALLYHEIGUE AND KERRY HEAD

Route information

Distance 17.5km (11 miles)

Grade Moderate

Terrain Good roads throughout. There are sections of steady climbing required.

Time to allow 1–2 hours.

Getting there by car Ballyheigue is on the north east corner of County Kerry, approximately 16km (10 miles) north west of Tralee on the R551. There is free on-street parking in the village.

Getting there by train There is no practical railway access to this route.

Starting from Ballyheigue, the route heads west running close to the coast with lovely views of the sea. The road gradually ascends as you head towards Kerry Head. The glorious sea views are maintained as the road heads east again with distant views of Loop Head and its lighthouse across the sea in County Clare. The final section of the route back to Ballyheigue involves a steep descent with distant views across Banna Strand.

Route description

Start from the green overlooking the sea next to the statue of Sir Roger Casement. With your back to the statue head L, SP Wave Crest Accommodation, passing the battlements of

Ballyheigue

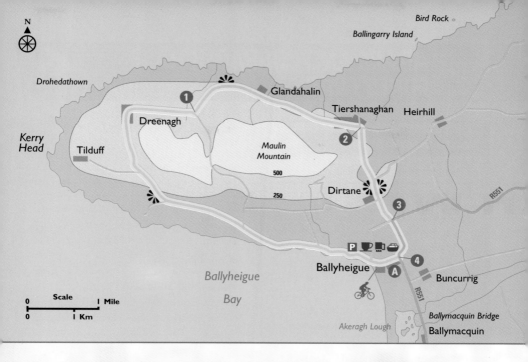

Ballyheigue Golf Club on RHS. Follow this road, passing the dead end turn to Kerry Head.

1 TL at TJ, SP Ballyheigue. **9.5km (6 miles)**

2 Bear R at XR, SP Ballyheigue.

3 TR at TJ along centrally lined road, SP Ballyheigue. **16km (10 miles)**

4 TR, SP Ballyheigue, and continue into village to finish the ride. **17.5km (11 miles)**

In 1916 he landed on Banna Strand (the 8km/ 5 mile stretch of sand south of Ballyheigue) from a German submarine planning to bring guns in for the Easter Rising. He was caught, deported to London and tried and executed. His body has since been returned to Ireland.

Places of interest along the route

A Ballyheigue

Ballyheigue is a small seaside resort. In summer visitors can swim off the sandy beach or take pony and trap rides around the beach. The statue by the beach is of Sir Roger Casement.

Food and drink

Ballyheigue has shops, pubs and cafés close to the beach.

ADARE AND CURRAGHCHASE FOREST PARK

Route information

Distance 19km (12 miles)

Grade Moderate

Terrain Good surfaces throughout, except for a short section of track in Curraghchase Forest Park, where there is the mild inconvenience of lifting bicycles over two gates.

Time to allow 2–3 hours.

Getting there by car Adare is approximately 19km (12 miles) south west of Limerick on the N21. There is on-street parking.

Getting there by train There is no practical railway access to this route.

From Adare the route heads north west, gradually climbing along quiet lanes. Three attractions are close. Celtic Park Gardens are an optional 1.5km (1 mile) from the main route as you pass Stonehall Farm and Curraghchase Forest Park is passed through en route. The route is completed as it started, on quiet lanes.

Route description

Start from the Tourist Office in the Heritage Centre. Head R for village centre. After 100m, TR at mini roundabout, SP Celtic Park and Garden.

1 TL, SP Celtic Park & Gardens/Stonehall Visitor Farm.

2 To visit Celtic Park and Gardens, TR at XR for 1.5km (1 mile).

Otherwise, TL at XR, SP Stonehall Visitor Farm.
8km (5 miles)

3 TL at XR, no SP. Enter Curraghchase Forest Park. Pass entrance cabin and cycle through woods. Follow this tarmac road all the way to the car park (ignore turn to caravan site). From car park, head along uphill track to R that leads towards ruined house, past a map of the forest park. Follow track around front of house on raised balcony and keep following track as it goes around other side. When track heads R towards an abandoned shed, ignore it and head SO towards ornamental gate in corner of field. Lift bike over this gate and over another in 20m. You are now on tarmac at a R angled bend – continue SO.

4 TL at TJ, no SP but telegraph line crosses road L to R and you pass yellow house on RHS (11km/7 miles). Later follow SP Adare and continue into village.

5 TL at TJ in centre of Adare, no SP. Cross roundabout and return to Tourist Office to finish the ride.
19km (12 miles)

Places of interest along the route

Ⓐ Adare
One of the prettiest villages in Ireland. Adare has a great deal to offer the visitor, for whom it unashamedly caters. A journey through the

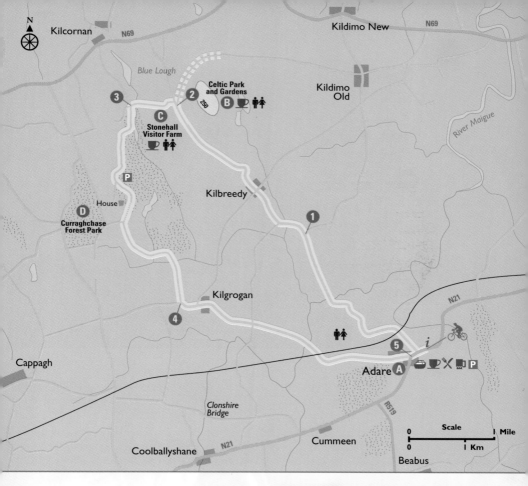

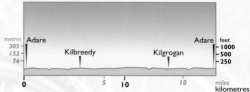

village's past is illustrated at the **Historical Exhibition** in Adare Heritage Centre. It is a good starting point as models and an audio-visual presentation help visitors to orientate themselves around the ruins of the village and also give an understanding as to how the Earls of Dunraven shaped the village. Open May to Sept, daily 0900–1700. Charge. Telephone (061) 396666. The Heritage Centre also houses craft outlets, a restaurant and the Tourist Office. Sited by the river, **Desmond Castle** was besieged by English forces in 1580 and Cromwell took possession of it in 1657. The castle has undergone restoration and is pic-turesque. There are two friaries in the village, the ruined Franciscan friary was founded in 1464 and the Augustinian friary was founded in 1316. Both are to the south of the village. Contact the Tourist Office for more information on (061) 396255.

Ⓑ **Celtic Park and Gardens, near Adare**

Located on an original Celtic settlement, the

Wild flowers

park and gardens illustrate the physical structures associated with Ireland's past. Some structures are original and include a stone circle, dolmen, cooking site and a surviving early stone fort. Also a classical style formal garden, containing roses, rockeries and herbaceous borders. Tearoom. Open mid March to October, daily 0930-1800. Charge. Telephone (061) 394243.

ⒸStonehall Visitor Farm, Curraghchase

Covering over 18ha (45 acres), the farm is home to a wide variety of both natural and exotic species. As well as cattle, deer, emus and a children's corner, there are bats present in the ruins of an old stone cottage and they can be viewed up close. Also indoor children's play area and nature walks around the farm. Tearoom. Open April to September, Monday–Saturday 1000–1800, Sunday 1200–1800; October to March, Sunday only. Charge. Telephone (061) 393940.

ⒹCurraghchase Forest Park, Curraghchase

The park is owned by the Irish Forestry Board and comprises 250ha (618 acres). There are forest walks, a large lake, nature trails and an arboretum. The most striking feature is the ruin of Curraghchase House. This large residence was home to the De Vere family for over 300 years. Anthony De Vere was a well-know author and poet in the 19th century. Unfortunately, the house was gutted by fire in 1941 and today only the shell remains. Open all year, daily during daylight hours. Free access if on a bicycle.

Food and drink

Plenty of choice in Adare. Refreshments are available at Celtic Park and Gardens and Stonehall Visitor Centre.

LOUGH GUR

Route information

Distance 20km (12.5 miles)

Grade Moderate

Terrain Mostly quiet, undulating lanes — some are narrow and the surface a little poor and there are a few short, steep climbs involved. There are two junctions at the start and finish of the route where special care must be taken.

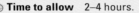

Time to allow 2–4 hours.

Getting there by car Herbertstown is a quiet village approximately 19km (12 miles) south of Limerick on the R513. There is plenty of on-street parking.

Getting there by train There is no practical railway access to this route.

From the tiny village of Herbertstown, the route circuits Lough Gur and its historical artifacts, including a wedge tomb, ruined church and stone circle. The last section of the route leads past the Lough Gur Interpretative Centre, a good spot for a picnic with the best views of the lake.

Places of interest along the route

A Wedge Tomb, Lough Gur

Built as a communal grave, the well-preserved wedge tomb comprises a wall of smaller rocks supporting a large flat one on top. Originally these larger stones would have been covered by smaller stones. Although this tomb is not in the best of conditions, probably because it has been lived in, it is still a good example of this type of tomb. It was excavated in 1938 and the bones of at least eight adults and children were found. Free access at all reasonable times.

B Grange Stone Circle, Lough Gur

Comprising 113 stones, Grange Stone Circle is the largest such circle in Ireland. It was built circa 2000 BC by the Bronze Age people living around the lake. The circle's function is obscure, but as with most other circles it was probably religious given that the sun shines directly through the narrow entrance passageway on Midsummer's morning. Access is free but a donation is requested.

C Lough Gur

The first farmers arrived at Lough Gur in circa 3000 BC. They cleared the forest, built stone houses and planted crops. A slide show at the Interpretative Centre details the geography and history of the lough and includes details of some of the finds made in the area. The most spectacular of these was a bronze shield found in the lake in the last century. A replica is on view (the original, as with most Irish artifacts, is in the National Museum, Dublin) along with pottery and axe heads. Picnic area on the lough shores. Open May to September, daily 1000–1800. Charge. Telephone (061) 361511.

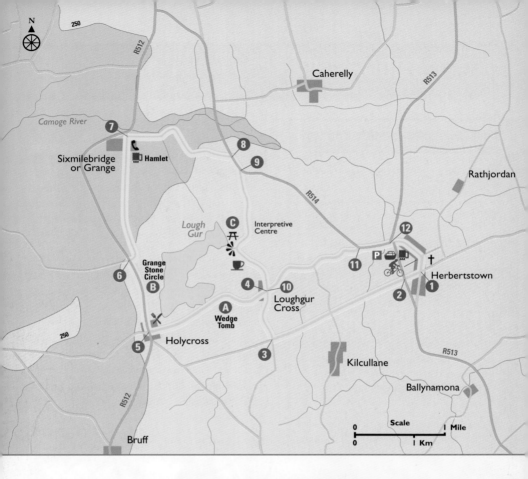

Route description

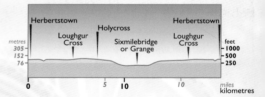

Start opposite light pink church in centre of Herbertstown. Head downhill, away from water tower.

1 TR at XR, no SP (SO SP Hospital). Descend and take CARE at next junction.

2 SO at XR, SP Holycross/Croom.

3 TR at XR, SP Lough Gur. *3km (2 miles)*

4 TL at XR, SP Holycross/Croom. Standing stone on RHS of junction. Pass wedge tomb on LHS.

5 TR at XR, SP Limerick. Pass stone circle on RHS.

6 TR at XR, SP Grange Church.
8km (5 miles)

7 TR next to Hamlet pub, no SP. Pass to R of telephone box at junction.

8   TR at TJ along centrally lined road, no SP.
13.5km (8.5 miles)

9   TR, SP Lough Gur Visitor Centre.

10   TL at XR, SP Herbertstown.
16.5km (10.5 miles)

11   TR at TJ onto centrally lined road, no SP. Take CARE at next junction.

12   SO at XR, no SP. Enter Herbertstown and finish ride.   **20km (12.5 miles)**

Food and drink

Herbertstown has one shop and a pub. There is a garage and restaurant at Holycross, a pub at Sixmilebridge and a café (tea, coffee, ice cream and outdoor seating) just past the entrance for Lough Gur Interpretative Centre.

Lough Gur

RINGASKIDDY AND CORK

Route information

Distance   21km (13 miles)

Grade   Easy

Terrain   Good quality roads throughout.

Time to allow   1–2 hours.

Getting there by car   Ringaskiddy is south east of Cork on the N28. There is a car park in the town.

Getting there by train   There is no practical railway access to this route.

Getting there by ferry   Swansea–Cork ferries run a daily service during the summer months. Telephone (021) 271166 or visit www.swansea-cork.ie

A large number of cyclists arrive in County Cork on the ferry. This route has been written to provide the most scenic way into Cork, whilst at the same time providing an opportunity to visit the pretty town of Cobh.

Food and drink

Plenty of choice in Cobh and Cork. There are pubs in Ringaskiddy, Monkstown and Passage West.

Shamrock Bar
A bar and, across the road, a shop.

Route description

Exit the ferry terminal.

1   TR at TJ along N28, SP All Routes.

2   SO at roundabout, SP All routes. Immediately TR, no SP, and pass between the Shamrock Bar and the Shamrock Stores. Descend.

3   TR at TJ, no SP but SP on LHS to ferry/ R609 (5km/3 miles). Pass ferry on RHS. To visit Cobh, take short ferry ride across to Great Island. TR at other side and follow road into Cobh.

Otherwise, continue through Passage West and towards Cork.

4   SO at XR (roundabout), SP Douglas/R610.

5   TR at roundabout, SP Douglas (16.5km/ 10.5 miles). SO at roundabout by Dunnes Stores.

6   TR at roundabout, SP Cork. Pass under bridge to SO at XR (traffic lights), no SP. Pass SP City Centre 4km on LHS. Continue SO, passing through sets of traffic lights. Just after passing hospital on LHS:

7   TR, SP All Routes, descend to:

8   SO at XR (traffic lights) along Infirmary Road, no SP. Bear L, SP All Routes, into one-way system. Continue through traffic lights to follow river on RHS. Bear R, crossing stone bridge to bear L, SP West Cork/ Killarney/ Blarney. Follow road to memorial and Tourist Office on RHS to finish the ride.

21km (13 miles)

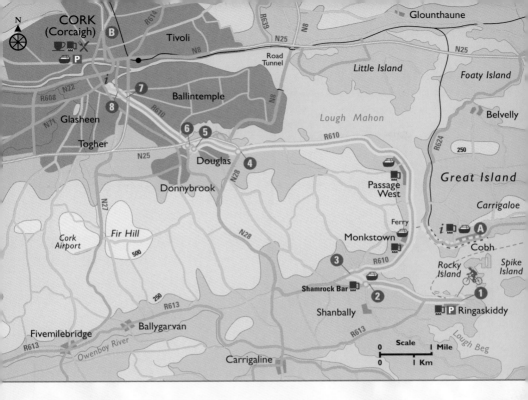

Places of interest along the route

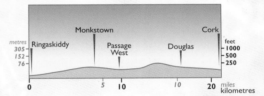

Chart labels: metres 305 152 76 / feet 1000 500 250; Ringaskiddy, Monkstown, Passage West, Douglas, Cork; 0 ... 5 ... 10 ... 10 ... 20 miles kilometres

A Cobh

Famous as the last stopping place of the Titanic, Cobh is a pretty town — a holiday resort and still used harbour to a large fishing fleet. A recent addition to Cobh was the beautiful **St Colman's Cathedral**, completed in 1915 using money donated by Irish Communities in America and Australia. It contains the largest carillon in Ireland at 47 bells, with the largest weighing 3440kg. **Cobh Heritage Centre** describes the town's history. Situated in the old railway station, there are excellent and informative displays on mass emigrations to America, the Titanic and many other stories of the sea. Coffee shop. Open March to December, daily 1000–1800. Charge. Another smaller museum is sited in the 19th-century **Scots Presbyterian Church**. Open April to September, Monday–Saturday 1100–1300 and 1400–1800, Sunday 1500–1800. For more information contact the Tourist Office on (021) 813301.

B Cork

Ireland's second largest conurbation. Dating back to the 7th century, it has played a major role in the struggle for independence. The Black and Tans killed the mayor in 1920 and many of the city's buildings were burnt down during the Anglo-Irish war. Today Cork is a bustling city, much of it new but with glimpses of its well-preserved remaining architectural heritage. **Cork Public Museum**, Fitzgerald Park, contains exhibits related to Cork with emphasis on the civic regalia and trades and crafts of the 19th and 20th centuries. Open all year, Monday–Friday 1100–1300 and 1415–1800, Sunday 1500–1700. Admission free. **Cork City Gaol** is housed in a castle. Opened in 1824, today it is a tourist attraction. A taped tour starts in the Governor's Office and leads you through the refurbished cells with life-sized figures and original graffiti. Open all year, daily March to October 0930–1800; November to February 1000–1700. Charge. Above the gaol is the **National Radio Museum**, home to a radio collection and a permanent exhibition dealing with Marconi and the birth of radio. Charge. There is much else to see in Cork. Contact the Tourist Office for more information on (021) 273251.

Statue of Emigrants to America, Cobh

CORK AND BLARNEY CASTLE

Route information

Distance   22.5km (14 miles)

Grade   Moderate

Terrain   Good roads throughout although the climb out of Cork is quite long. Traffic in Cork is busy, so please take care.

Time to allow   2–3 hours.

Getting there by car   Cork, one of Ireland's major cities, can be reached from the N20, N22, N25 and the N8. There are several car parks in the city. The route starts from the Tourist Office.

Getting there by train   There are regular services to Cork Station. For information telephone (1850) 366222 or visit www.irishrail.ie

Starting from the centre of Cork, the route climbs west out of the city, via the Butter Museum. After the climb, the route descends almost all the way to Blarney. From Blarney, the route heads west and then south, returning to Cork via the attractive valley of the River Lee.

Places of interest along the route

Ⓐ Cork

Ireland's second largest city. See Route 4 for more information.

Ⓑ Blarney Castle

Dating from 1446, Blarney Castle is one of the most visited sites in Ireland. The Blarney Stone is the main draw. Having ascended a spiral staircase, visitors must bend over backwards to kiss the sacred rock accompanied by the gentle verbal patter from a helping local. Tradition says that in return the rock has the power to confer eloquence! Refreshments available. Open all year, Monday–Saturday 0930–1830, Sunday 0930–1730. Charge. Telephone (021) 385252; www.blarneycastle.ie

Route description

To start from the railway station, TL out of station onto Lower Glanmire road and continue along this road, SO at all junctions (MacCurtain Street/Coburg Street/Devonshire Street). Arrive at junction with John Street Upper and pick up route at direction 3 where SO then bear R in front of Butter Museum.

To start from Cork Tourist Office, head right along dual carriageway (Grand Parade) towards city centre. Continue SO at traffic lights, SP Dublin/Waterford. Stay on this road (becomes Saint Patrick's Street), SO through several sets of traffic lights, passing shops on either side, until you arrive at junction opposite St Patrick's Bridge over river.

1   TL at XR, SP Blarney/Shandon. Cross next bridge (Christy Ring Bridge), following SP Blarney. On other side of bridge:

2   TL at XR, SP Gurranabraher/ Knocknaheeney. Follow further SP to these places as road bears R.

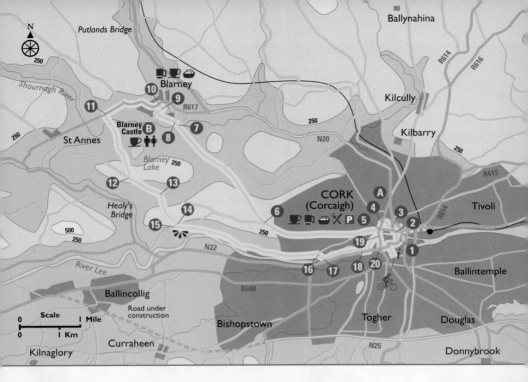

3 TL, SP Shandon (ignore Blarney SP pointing R). Follow road towards Shandon centre and bear R in front of Butter Museum. Then bear L in front of St Ann's Church.

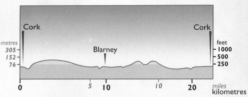

4 TL at XR, no SP (pedestrian crossing RHS). Descend.

5 Take first TR, no SP, along Blarney Street. Climb to leave city.

6 TR, SP Blarney. **5km (3 miles)**

7 TL, SP Blarney.

8 TL, SP Blarney Castle/Parking (9km/5.5 miles). Continue to castle entrance. On return from entrance:

9 TL at TJ, no SP. Pass Blarney Castle Hotel on RHS.

10 TL at TJ, SP Ballincollig Tower.

11 TL, SP Kerry Pike. Climb.

12 TL at TJ, SP O'Sullivan Nursery and Plant Centre. Pass nursery and plant centre on LHS.

13 TR, no SP (opposite stone cross memorial). **14.5km (9 miles)**

14 TR at TJ, no SP (wall opposite). Descend.

15 TL at TJ along centrally lined road, no SP (wall opposite). Pass several attractive sequential stone monuments on LHS.

16 TR, SP Killarney/West Cork/City Centre. Cross river.

17 TL, SP brown bike. Pass between railings (sports pitches on LHS).

18 TL at TJ (effectively SO), no SP, onto busier road. Bear L, SP Limerick.

21km (13 miles)

19 TR at XR, no SP. Pass Gate Multiplex at junction on RHS. Pass Dunnes Stores on LHS.

Food and drink

There is lots of choice for refreshment in Cork and in Blarney village. Refreshments are also available at Blarney Castle.

20 TL at XR along Washington Street, no SP. At end, TR at TJ, SP South Ring, and return to Tourist Office to finish the ride.

22.5km (14 miles)

Cork

ROSSCARBERY AND GLANDORE

Route information

Distance   23km (14.5 miles)

Grade   Strenuous

Terrain   The back lanes out of Rosscarbery are rough in places, after which the surface improves. There are several steep climbs, one of which is also long.

Time to allow   2–4 hours.

Getting there by car   Rosscarbery is on just off the N71 Clonakilty/ Skibbereen road. After crossing bridge, follow SP Village Centre, where there is on-street parking.

Getting there by train   There is no practical railway access to this route.

From the village of Rosscarbery, the route heads west, climbing and descending through quiet lanes, to pass the scenic ruin of Coppinger's Court. Not far away is Drombeg Stone Circle, passed en route. There are opportunities for lovely views of Rabbit Island and Adams Island on the way into Glandore. The route runs alongside Glandore harbour and on to Leap, on the busy N71. The return route to Rosscarbery follows quiet though hilly lanes. Contact the Tourist Office at Clonakilty for more information on (023) 33226.

Places of interest along the route

Ⓐ Rosscarbery

St Fachtna founded a monastery at Rosscarbery, at the head of an inlet, during the 6th century. The monastery soon became a celebrated seat of learning for many families in the area and the cathedral remains can be seen today, with an elaborately carved western doorway dating from the 12th century. O'Donovan Rossa was born in the village in 1832. He came to prominence as a founder of the Fenian movement which supported independence for Ireland through violence.

Ⓑ Coppinger's Court, near Rosscarbery

Built in the 17th century by Sir Walter Coppinger, Coppinger's Court is now a roofless ruin, having been attacked and burnt down during the 1641 rebellion. Free access at time of writing, although this may be restricted in the future.

Ⓒ Drombeg Stone Circle, near Rosscarbery

Dating from 100BC, Drombeg Stone Circle comprises 17 stones set in beautiful surroundings. The axis of a recumbent stone to the south west and two taller stones to the north east line up to the midwinter sunset. The site was excavated in 1957, when a central pit containing the ground up cremated remains of an adolescent was discovered. Radio carbon dating revealed a date of 600AD. To the western side of the site are two huts, containing a well and a trough in which water was boiled to cook meat. This cooking site predates the rest of the remains by 200 years, and may have been a seasonal resting site for hunters. Information kiosk. Free access at all reasonable times.

D Glandore

Overlooking a pretty harbour, Glandore is a popular stop for boats and yachts touring the southern coast of Ireland. Glandore was originally set up at the end of the 17th century by William Thompson, as a commune for socialist philosophy, advocating equality for women and mass education.

Food and drink

There are shops and pubs in Rosscarbery, Leap and Glandore, where there is also a tearoom.

Coppinger's Court

Route description

Start from the foot of the main street in Rosscarbery, next to old SP Abbey Bar/Clonakilty/Reenascreena/O'Sullivans Family Butcher. Head up short street towards pharmacy and SP Skibbereen. Bear L at top, past telephone box on RHS. Take first TR and descend steeply towards playing fields.

1 SO at XR, SP Glandore/Union Hall.

2 TL, SP Curraheen Lodge Hostel. Climb narrow lane.

3 TR at TJ, no SP (low stone wall on LHS).

1.5km (1 mile)

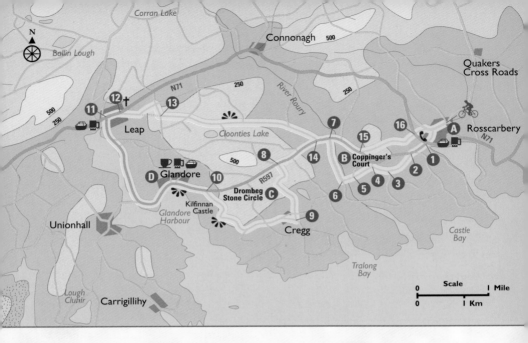

4 TL at TJ, no SP (short driveway opposite) – CARE as steep descent. If TR in error here, you will descend to centrally lined road.

5 TL at TJ (effectively SO), no SP. Shortly afterwards, cross bridge to:

6 TR at TJ, no SP (river on RHS). Continue, passing Coppinger's Court on RHS.

7 TL at TJ along centrally lined road, no SP (bridge over River Roury on RHS).

8 TL, SP Drombeg Stone Circle. Descend past circle.

9 TR at TJ, no SP (telegraph poles on LHS).
6.5km (4 miles)

10 TL at TJ, no SP (Kilfinnan Castle on LHS). Follow road through Glandore.

11 TR at TJ along centrally lined road, no

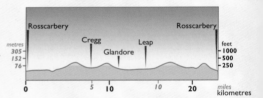

SP (other direction SP Skibbereen). Just before large church on LHS:

12 TR, no SP, for steep climb.
15km (9.5 miles)

13 TL, no SP (high hedge on LHS). Pass farm entrance with cattle grid on LHS. Keep climbing!

14 TL at TJ, no SP. Cross River Roury.

15 TL, no SP.

16 SO at XR, no SP, into Rosscarbery to finish the ride.
23km (14.5 miles)

GOLEEN AND MIZEN HEAD

Route information

Distance   25.5km (16 miles)

Grade   Moderate

Terrain   Good quality roads with a few steady climbs.

Time to allow   2–3 hours.

Getting there by car   Goleen is on the R591 Bantry/Crookhaven road. There is on-street parking in the village.

Getting there by train   There is no practical railway access to this route.

Starting from Goleen, the route heads west towards Ireland's most southwesterly point – Mizen Head. Heading along the coast road you will see Crookhaven village across Crook Haven and, if you wish, you can take a diversion to visit. The route, however, continues past the lovely beach of Barley Cove (good views). Turning south west the route heads along the dead end road to Mizen Head, where the now automated lighthouse can be visited. The outward route is partially retraced before a gentle climb and descent take you back to Goleen.

Places of interest along the route

A Crookhaven

As the southernmost village in Ireland, Crookhaven was an important port in the age of sail, due to its sheltered position. As well as supporting a thriving fishing industry during the 19th century, the village also provided the first port of call for many transatlantic ships. Today it is the leisure sailing industry that keeps this village alive.

B Barley Cove

Probably the best beach in west Cork, and popular with surfers. Barley Cove is a safe sandy area, patrolled by lifeguards in the summer. Behind the beach is Lissagriffin, a large shallow lough important as a stop over and feeding area for large numbers of migrating wading birds. In winter the lough is home to ducks and swans. There are plenty of interpretive signs to explain the wildlife that can be seen in the area.

C Mizen Head

With soaring cliffs and a wide variety of seabirds, Mizen Head is Ireland's most southwesterly point. It was from here that Marconi sent his first transatlantic signal to America. The Mizen Head Signal Station was completed in 1910 and this along with the Fastnet provided safe passage for ships. In 1993 the station was automated. Today a visitor centre allows visitors to walk to the head and lighthouse across a high, single span bridge. Although the lighthouse is not tall (the cliffs were deemed high enough), there are rooms full of memorabilia, allowing a good appreciation of what life would have been like when the station was manned. Café. Open mid March, April, May and October, daily 1030–1700; June to September, daily 1000–1800; November to mid March, weekends 1100–1600. Telephone (028) 35591/ 35225; www.mizenvision.com

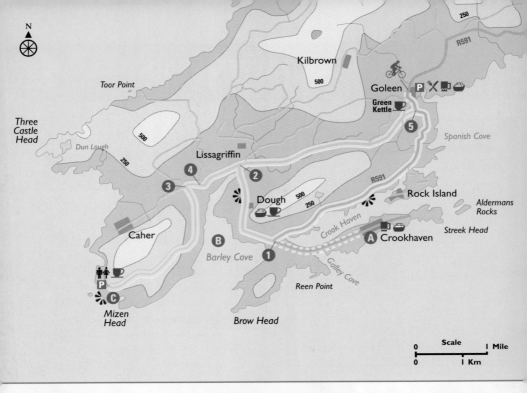

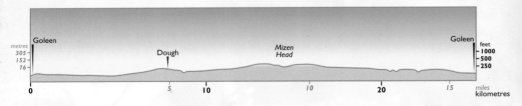

Route description

Start from Mizen Tourism Cooperative Society at east end of Goleen. Head through village, following R591.

1 To visit Crookhaven, continue SO.

Otherwise, TR, SP Barley Cove/Mizen Head. Pass Barley Cove on LHS.

2 TL at TJ, SP Mizen Head. *9.5km (6 miles)*

3 TL and follow this road as far as Mizen Head car park (14.5km/9 miles). After visit, retrace route to direction 4.

4 TR at TJ, no SP but telegraph lines on RHS (19km/12 miles). Continue SO along this road towards Goleen.

5 TL at TJ, SP Schull/Ballydehob/Bantry/Skibbereen. Continue into Goleen to finish the ride. *25.5km (16 miles)*

Food and drink

There are pubs and shops in Goleen and Crookhaven. Barleycove Caravan Park has a shop and a café, and refreshments are available at Mizen Head visitor centre.

Green Kettle, Goleen
At the start and finish of the route.

Barley Cove from Mizen Head

SKIBBEREEN AND BALTIMORE

Route information

Distance   26.5km (16.5 miles)

Grade   Moderate

Terrain   Reasonable surfaces throughout. There is a hard zig-zag climb away from Lough Hyne.

Time to allow   2–3 hours.

Getting there by car   Skibbereen is on the N71. There is a car park as well as on-street parking.

Getting there by train   There is no practical railway access to this route.

From Skibbereen the route heads south west along back lanes to the marine reserve of Lough Hyne, where it is possible to cycle along the lough shore and/or swim in its warm waters. A hard climb leads away from the lough, with the reward of a descent to the outskirts of Baltimore. The return to Skibbereen illustrates the rocky interior, where small cottages seem to be hidden in between the land and the rocky shore of the Ilen estuary.

Places of interest along the route

A Skibbereen

Considered the major centre of west Cork, Skibbereen was founded by English settlers when in 1631 Algerian pirates raided Baltimore

to the west. Skibbereen was badly affected by the famine of the 1840s, when the local potato crop failed. Many victims were buried in a communal grave in the local Abbey cemetery. A leaflet describing the Skibbereen Trail – sites linked with the famine – can be purchased from some of the local shops. In the centre of the town is a statue of the Maid of Erin, erected in 1904 to commemorate the Irish rebellions of 1798, 1803, 1848 and 1867. Skibbereen Heritage Centre contains displays on the Great Famine and an interpretive centre for Lough Hyne. Open mid March to mid Sept, Tuesday–Saturday 1000–1800. Charge. Telephone (028) 40900 or visit www.skibbheritage.com. Regular art exhibitions and musicals are held at the West Cork Arts Centre in North Street. For more information contact the Tourist Office on (028) 21766; www.skibbereen.ie

B Lough Hyne

Situated on the coast between Skibbereen and Baltimore, Lough Hyne is a lovely example of one of the few sea loughs in Ireland. In 1981 the lough became Ireland's first Marine Nature Reserve. Measuring 3/4km wide and 1km long, the lough is 55m deep in places. It is fed from the Atlantic via Barloge Creek, where the water can flow in and out at up to 16km (10 miles) an hour. More than 1000 species of sealife have been found in the lough, including purple sea urchins and sea slugs, which can be seen grazing in the shallow waters.

C Baltimore

Baltimore lies at the mouth of the River Ilen. It was once the stronghold of the O'Driscoll clan and one of their castles dominates the harbour. In 1537 men from Waterford made a revenge

Baltimore Harbour

attack on the O'Driscolls and set fire to the town and the castle. Baltimore's population was further reduced in 1631, when Algerian pirates removed over 100 people, taking them back to north Africa. Today the summer population swells as people arrive on boats to sail and dive in the local waters. Boat trips to Clear, Sherkin and Hair Islands are available from the harbour. Contact the Tourist Office at Skibbereen for more information.

Route description

Start from the Tourist Office. Head the short distance into town to immediately bear L, SP All Routes, passing statue on LHS. Immediately take RHF, SP N71 (written on ground), passing post office on LHS. Cross pedestrian crossing.

1 SO at XR (roundabout), SP Baltimore.

2 TL at XR, SP Evans Engineering (stone cross memorial and seat to right of junction).

3 TR, no SP (house with flying bird statues on LHS).

4 SO at XR, no SP. Follow lane as it bears R then L.

5 TL at TJ, no SP. Pass Lough Hyne and access to lough shores. Continue for hard, zig-zag climb.

6 LHF, no SP (two telegraph poles on RHS).
9km (5.5 miles)

7 TL at TJ onto centrally lined road, no SP. Enter Baltimore and follow one-way system past harbour.

8 TL at TJ, SP Skibbereen.

9 TR at TJ, SP Skibbereen. Continue, passing Old Court Inn.

10 TL, effectively SO, SP Ballydehob.

11 TR at TJ, no SP (other direction crosses bridge).

12 TR at TJ, effectively SO, SP Clonakilty/Cork. Follow one-way system back to Skibbereen Tourist Office to finish the ride.
26.5km (16.5 miles)

Food and drink

Lots of choice in Skibbereen and Baltimore.

Old Court Inn, near Skibbereen
Passed on the return to Skibbereen.

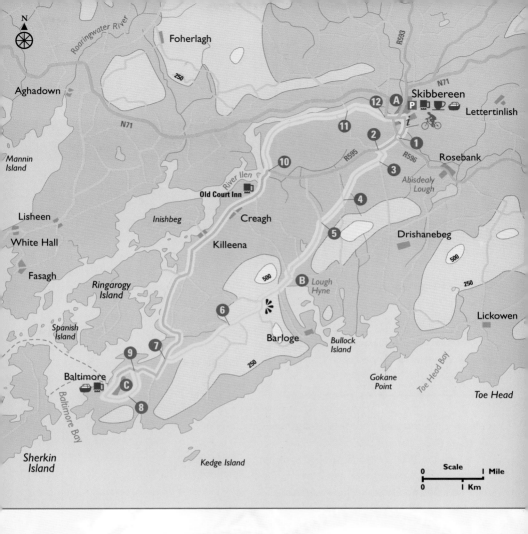

N

Roaringwater River

Foherlagh

R593

N71

Skibbereen

12 A P

Lettertinlish

Aghadown

N71

11

2

1

250

Mannin
Island

River Ilen

10

R595

3

R596

Rosebank

Abisdealy
Lough

Old Court Inn

Lisheen

Inishbeg

Creagh

4

5

Drishanebeg

500

White Hall

Killeena

250

Fasagh

Ringarogy
Island

500

B Lough
Hyne

Lickowen

Spanish
Island

6

Barloge

Bullock
Island

9

7

Toe Head Bay

Baltimore

250

Gokane
Point

C

8

Toe Head

Baltimore Bay

Sherkin
Island

Kedge Island

Scale

0   1 Mile

0   1 Km

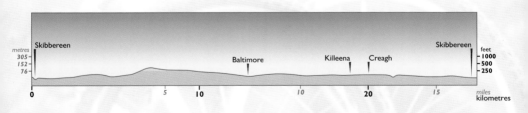

metres
305
152
76

Skibbereen

Baltimore

Killeena

Creagh

Skibbereen

feet
1000
500
250

5   10   10   15

miles
kilometres

Route information

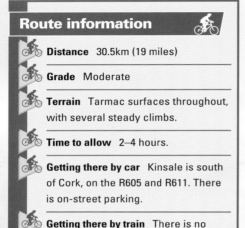

Distance 30.5km (19 miles)

Grade Moderate

Terrain Tarmac surfaces throughout, with several steady climbs.

Time to allow 2–4 hours.

Getting there by car Kinsale is south of Cork, on the R605 and R611. There is on-street parking.

Getting there by train There is no practical railway access to this route.

From Kinsale the route heads south to cross the River Bandon and skirt scenic Sandy Cove. On to join the R604, towards the Old Head of Kinsale. There are wonderful sea views as the route reaches the most southerly point of this spit of land, where the old head is joined to the mainland. Unfortunately the construction of a golf course has denied access to the head itself. The route turns north to the blue flag beaches Garrylucas and on through Ballinspittle, the location of an enormous grotto, before returning to Kinsale via back roads with panoramic views of Kinsale harbour.

Places of interest along the route

Ⓐ Kinsale

Scenically pretty Kinsale is famed for its seafood restaurants and the town holds a gourmet festival in mid October. The town has two museums. In Market Square there is a **museum** relating the story of the sinking of the *Lusitania*. Open July and August. Charge. In Cork Street, **Desmond Castle** houses a small museum on the history of wine. Open mid April to mid September, 0900–1800 (closed each Monday, April to mid June). Charge. Telephone (021) 4774855. A short distance to the east of Kinsale is **Charles Fort**. The fort was built in the 1670s and most of it was destroyed as the British withdrew in 1921. However, despite this, it remains as one of the best preserved star forts in Europe. Tearoom. Open Easter to May and October, 0900–1700; June to September, 0900–1800. Charge. Telephone (021) 4772263. Contact the Tourist Office for more information on (021) 772234.

Ⓑ *Lusitania* Memorial

On 1 May, 1915, the *Lusitania* left New York with 1959 passengers onboard, bound for Europe. On 7 May, off Seven Heads on the coast of Ireland, she was torpedoed by a German U-boat. The ship sank in 18 minutes and 1198 people were drowned. The memorial is a simple one, noting the fact that the loss of

Old Head of Kinsale

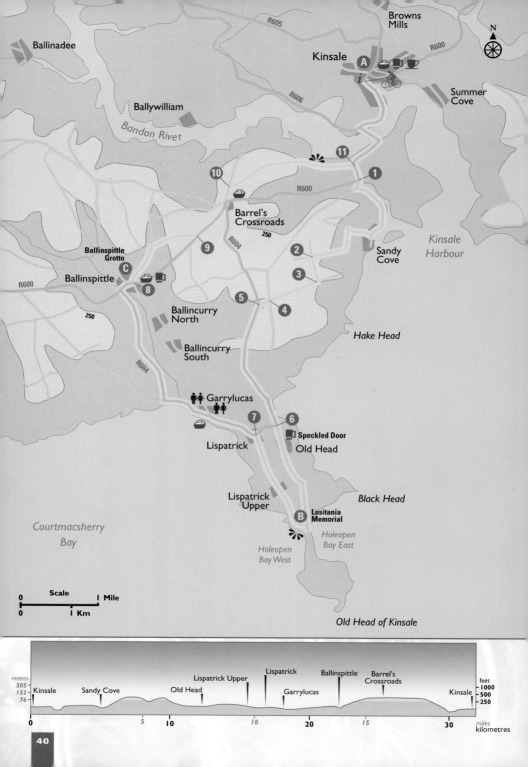

Ballinadee

Browns Mills

Kinsale

R605

R600

R606

Summer Cove

Ballywilliam

Bandon River

N

A
i

R600

11

10

Barrel's
Crossroads

R600

1

R604

250

2

Sandy
Cove

Kinsale
Harbour

Ballinspittle
Grotto

R600

Ballinspittle

C

9

3

8

5

4

Ballincurry
North

Hake Head

250

Ballincurry
South

R604

Garrylucas

7

6

Speckled Door

Old Head

Lispatrick

Lispatrick
Upper

Black Head

Courtmacsherry
Bay

B Lusitania
Memorial

Holeopen
Bay East

Holeopen
Bay West

Old Head of Kinsale

Scale
0 _____ 1 Mile
0 _____ 1 Km

metres
305
152
76

Kinsale   Sandy Cove   Old Head   Lispatrick Upper   Lispatrick   Ballinspittle   Barrel's
Crossroads   Kinsale

Garrylucas

feet
1000
500
250

0   5   10   20   15   30

miles
kilometres

123 US citizens on the *Lusitania* went some way to changing American public opinion to Allied forces during World War I.

🄲 Ballinspittle Grotto

The large roadside grotto at Ballinspittle is dedicated to Our Lady and St Bernadette and was blessed in 1954. The grotto is lovingly looked after and is striking because of the large blue letters reading 'I am the Immaculate Conception' that form the front wall. The grotto was briefly famous in the summer of 1985 when it attracted thousands of people after claims that the statue of the Virgin Mary had moved.

Route description

Start from the Tourist Office and head L, SP Bandon/Garrettstown. Pass marina on LHS and follow more of these SP as you bear L and leave town. Cross bridge following SP Coast Road/West Cork/Old Head.

1   TL, SP Sandy Cove. Follow this SP again as road bears R, and descend to picturesque cove.

2   TL at XR, no SP (opposite small abandoned quarry). Descend briefly then climb.

3   TL at TJ, no SP. (If TL, continue to end of cul-de-sac, descend path on left to reach pretty ruined church above cliffs).

4   SO at XR, SP Garrettstown.   ***8km (5 miles)***

5   TL at TJ, effectively SO, no SP (other direction SP Kinsale).

6   TL, effectively SO, no SP (Speckled Door pub on LHS). Follow this road around to Old Head – good cliff views if descend to R of golf club entrance.

7   TL at TJ, effectively SO, no SP (16km/ 10 miles). Pass Garrylucas beach on LHS. Pass second beach, head inland and cycle through Ballinspittle.

8   TR just before grotto, no SP. Climb.

9   TL at TJ, no SP (24km/15 miles). Descend to SO at staggered XR, SP Old Bridge Road. Pass shop on RHS.

10   RHF, no SP, for gentle climb. Descend, with good views of Kinsale ahead.

11   TL at TJ, SP River View B&B. Cross bridge and return to Tourist Office to finish the ride.   ***30.5km (19 miles)***

Food and drink

Plenty of choice in Kinsale. There is a beach shop in Garrylucas and shops and pubs in Ballinspittle.

Speckled Door pub, Old Head
Almost half-way along the route.

TRALEE, FENIT AND ARDFERT

Route information

Distance   34.5km (21.5 miles)

Grade   Easy

Terrain   Generally well graded roads, although the road out of Tralee is a little rough. The road between Ardfert and Tralee can be busy.

Time to allow   2–4 hours.

Getting there by car   Tralee is a large town on the N21, just north of the Dingle peninsula. There are several car parks in the town.

Getting there by train   There is a railway station at Tralee. For travel information telephone (1850) 366222 or visit www.irishrail.ie

From Tralee the route heads west along the northern edge of Tralee Bay to the seaside settlement of Fenit, where it is well worth visiting the pier to admire the boats and the solitary lighthouse in the bay. The north eastern section of the route gives pleasant views of Barrow Harbour and the sea beyond, before arriving at Ardfert, famed for its splendid ruined cathedral and associated churches. The return to Tralee follows the R551, which can be busy at times.

Places of interest along the route

Ⓐ Tralee

Tralee attracts attention each August when its annual festival culminates in the Rose of Tralee

each year, a beauty competition for pretty ladies of Irish origin from all over the world. Sited on the River Lee, Tralee is the capital of Kerry and was founded in 1216. The **Kerry County Museum** offers interactive displays and a trip in a time car to describe the sights and sounds of medieval Tralee. Also audio-visual tour of County Kerry. Café. Open mid March to December, daily 0930–1730; November and December, daily 1100–1630. Charge. Telephone (066) 7127777; www.kerrymuseum.com. The railway between Tralee and Dingle was closed in 1953 but a section has been relaid and an original engine restored as the **Tralee–Blennerville Light Railway**. Also in Tralee is the largest working windmill in Ireland, 18th-century **Blennerville Windmill**. Visitors can see the windmill in operation and exhibitions on the history of milling and emigration. Open April to October, daily. Telephone (066) 21064 to confirm times. For more information on the town and the surrounding area, telephone Tralee Tourist Office on (066) 7121288.

Ⓑ Fenit

The fishing village of Fenit was the birthplace of St Brendan the Navigator, a 1st-century monk who sailed around north west Europe spreading the Christian faith. The village's close links with the sea are well illustrated at **Fenit Seaworld**, located at the end of the pier. The aquarium has touch pools and a wave machine. Café. Open all year, daily 1000–1730 (during July and August closed 2000). Charge. Telephone (066) 36544.

Ⓒ Ardfert Cathedral, Ardfert

Dedicated to St Brendan the Navigator, Ardfert Cathedral dates from the 11th century, although the main construction dates from 1288–1336. As

Ardfert Cathedral

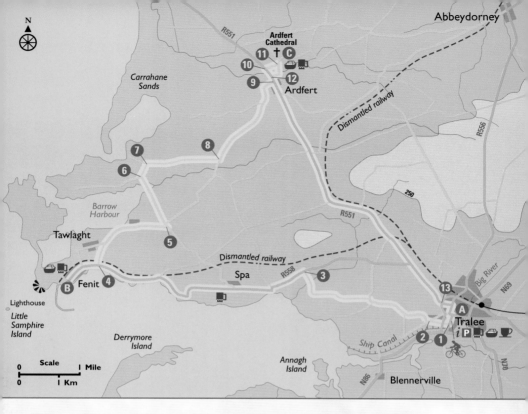

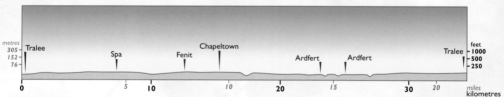

is the case with many religious buildings, the cathedral has been attacked, plundered and burned during its history, initially in 1152 and again in 1180. Today the various phases of construction can be seen. The main walls of the 13th-century cathedral are virtually intact and the most striking features are the nine trefoil headed lancet windows of the south wall, and the central window, one of the tallest in Ireland. Duchas property. Open June to early September, daily 1000–1800; early September to October, weekends 1000–1800. Charge. Telephone (066) 7134711; www.heritageireland.ie

Route description

Start from Tralee Tourist Office. Head L (park in front). Continue SO and follow SP Get in Lane/Dingle/The West.

1 TL at TJ, SP Dingle/Killorglin. Take next TR, SP The Kerries Golf Course. Then SO at XR, no SP, across Basin Road.

2 TL at TJ, no SP. Cross zebra crossing to immediately TR opposite hurling and football club, no SP.

3 TL at TJ onto centrally lined road, no SP (5km/3 miles). Continue into Fenit and onto quay. Retrace route out of Fenit and:

---

4 TL, SP The Lighthouse Hotel (14.5km/ 9 miles). Pass hotel on RHS.

---

5 TL, SP Tralee Golf Club/Sli Tour.

---

6 TR at TJ, SP Sli Tour.

---

7 TR at TJ, SP Sli Tour.

---

8 TL at TJ, SP Sli Tour/Ardfert/Ballyheigue.

---

9 TL at XR, SP Banna/Ballyheigue.
                              24km (15 miles)

---

10 TR, SP Cathedral.

---

11 Arrive opposite entrance to cathedral and TR, no SP.

12 TR at TJ, no SP, then immediately TL at TJ, SP Tralee. Continue along this road into Tralee.

---

13 SO at XR (traffic lights), SP Airport. TR at TJ opposite Market House and bear L. Then TR along Denny Street and finish the ride by the Tourist Office.   ***34.5km (21.5 miles)***

Food and drink

Lots of choice in Tralee. There are shops and pubs in Fenit and Ardfert. Refreshments are also available at Fenit Seaworld. Approximately half-way between Tralee and Fenit there is is a pub, behind which are two benches with great views across Tralee Bay.

Ardfert Churches and Cathedral Complex

Route 11

BALLYBUNNION AND CARRIGAFOYLE CASTLE

Route information

Distance   37.5km (23.5 miles)

Grade   Easy

Terrain   Quiet, reasonably surfaced lanes for most of the route.

Time to allow   2–4 hours.

Getting there by car   Ballybunnion is north west of Kerry, on the R551. There is on-street parking in town with free parking by the seafront. There are few opportunities for parking in the centre of town.

Getting there by train   There is no practical railway access to this route.

From the seaside resort of Ballybunnion the route heads inland, skirting the edge of Knockanore Mountain to the sea and Carrigafoyle Castle. Briefly heading inland through the village of Astee, the coastal views return as the route gets close to the coast on the return to Ballybunnion.

Places of interest along the route

A **Ballybunnion**

Situated by the sea, Ballybunnion is a popular holiday resort, with a sandy beach for swimming and surfing and the usual onshore entertainments. The beach is overlooked by a castle ruin, though apart from a single high wall little remains. Ballybunnion is well-know for golf, with the local courses holding many inter-national competitions. A statue commemorat-ing Bill Clinton's recent visit has immortalised him in a golfing pose. Seaweed baths have long been a part of local life and there are still several bathing houses in the town. Contact Tralee Tourist Office for more information on (066) 7221288.

B **Carrigafoyle Castle**

Standing on the Shannon estuary, Carrigafoyle Castle is one of the most impressive castles in Ireland. It was built by the O'Connors, reputed to be a ruthless family. Legend says that a daughter of the house had never seen a hanging – an unfortunate old man passing in his cart was brought in and hung for her entertainment. The castle was besieged on several occasions and a large section of the roof destroyed by cannon fire. However, inside, the ceiling is still of interest. It was built by laying wicker on a wooden stage. On top of this were laid stones, encased in mortar. When the mortar had set, the wooden stage was removed and a domed roof remained. Evidence of the wicker can still be seen today. Free access.

Carrigafoyle Castle

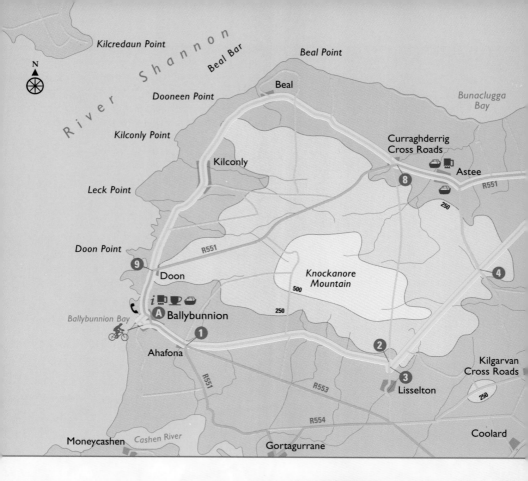

River Shannon

Kilcredaun Point

N

Beal Bar

Beal Point

Beal

Dooneen Point

Bunaclugga
Bay

Kilconly Point

Curraghderrig
Cross Roads

Kilconly

Astee

8

R551

250

Leck Point

R551

Knockanore
Mountain

500

Doon Point

9

Doon

4

i

A Ballybunnion

250

Ballybunnion Bay

1

2

Ahafona

3 Lisselton

Kilgarvan
Cross Roads

R551

R553

250

Moneycashen

Cashen River

R554

Coolard

Gortagurrane

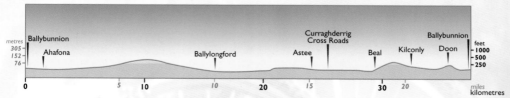

metres | Ballybunnion | | | | Curraghderrig | | | | Ballybunnion | feet
305 | Ahafona | | | Ballylongford | Cross Roads | | Beal | Kilconly | Doon | 1000
152 | | | | | | Astee | | | | 500
76 | | | | | | | | | | 250

0   5   10   10   20   15   30   20
miles
kilometres

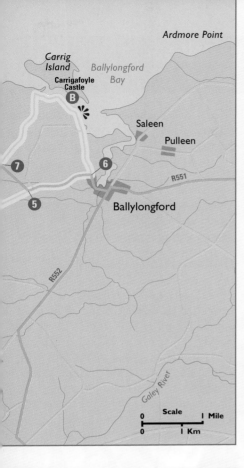

Food and drink

Lots of choice in Ballybunnion. There are a couple of shops and a pub in Astee.

Route description

Start next to the telephone boxes with your back to the sea close to the beach in Ballybunnion. Head R to immediately TL at TJ in front of Golf Hotel, no SP. Leave town passing Bill Clinton statue on LHS.

1 TL, no SP. Pass raised triangular area of grass with seat on RHS.

2 TR at TJ, no SP.

3 TL, no SP. **7km (4.5 miles)**

4 SO at XR, no SP (11km/7 miles). Pass Ballylongford community alert SP on LHS.

5 TR at TJ onto centrally lined road, no SP (large triangular grassed junction). Enter Ballylongford.

6 TL, SP Carrigafoyle Castle (16km/ 10 miles). Follow road past castle and then inland.

7 TR at TJ onto centrally lined road, no SP. Cycle through Astee.

8 TR, SP Coastal Drive/Coast Road.
 25.5km (16 miles)

9 TR at TJ, SP Sli Tour. Enter Ballybunnion to complete the ride. **37.5km (23.5 miles)**

DUNQUIN AND THE DINGLE PENINSULA

Route information

 Distance   40km (25 miles)

Grade   Moderate

Terrain   There is one hard climb and a short section of riding across a beach. Even if the tide is in, the sand is firm!

Time to allow   3–5 hours.

Getting there by car   Dunquin is the most easterly village on the Dingle peninsula, on the R559. There is parking at the Great Blasket Centre, which is well signed.

Getting there by train   There is no practical railway access to this route.

Starting from the Great Blasket Centre in Dunquin, the route heads inland, climbing away from the sea (look behind for expansive views of the Blasket Islands). The route descends, latterly along a tarmac track, to Ballyferriter and on along lanes to a lonely beach overlooking Smerwick Harbour. The route turns inland again, over a small pass to Ventry. The final section of the route back to Dunquin is the loveliest – a ride around Slea Head with plenty of glorious sea views and ancient history along the way. There are a lot of things to look at en route around Slea Head. Some are well-signed and regulated (admission charge, etc signposted); others are less so. You can see all these attractions from the road.

Places of interest along the route

A **The Blasket Centre, Dunquin**
The centre, opened in 1993, describes the history and culture of Great Blasket Island through the remarkable accounts of the community that last lived there in 1953. The residents spoke little English and in their isolation wrote numerous stories and poetry. This is all brought to life by an audio visual display and a good collection of photographs. The islands themselves can be seen from the centre (Great Blasket is the largest). Café. Duchas site. Open Easter to September, daily 1000–1800. Charge. Telephone (066) 56444.

B **Ballyferriter**
Named after the Ferriter family whose son Piaras fought in the rebellion of 1642, Ballyferriter is a pretty little village with a church and a Heritage Museum describing local history. Free admission to café; charge for museum. Telephone (066) 56100 to confirm opening times.

C **Fort Del Oro**
Set into the sea, Fort Del Oro has a beautiful panoramic view of the sea and mountains of Dingle. It was the site of a brutal massacre in 1580, when English forces besieged Spanish,

Dingle Bay

Italian and Irish forces inside the castle. Today the raised walls of earth can still be seen. Free access at all reasonable times.

D Celtic and Prehistoric Museum, near Dunquin

With a good degree of comic touch the large guide to the Celtic and Prehistoric Museum leads you through the centuries from Palaeolithic times, through the Bronze Age to Celtic times. Many artifacts in excellent condition from all over Europe are displayed. Pride of place goes to Millie, a huge mammoth skull. The café contains seating from churches and 1950s American cars and offers views across the bay. Open May to September, daily 0930–1730. Charge. Telephone (066) 9159941; www.kerryweb.ie

E Dunbeg

The ancient promontory fort at Dunbeg is well preserved – there are still four earthen defence rings and within these, the remains of a dwelling.

F Beehive Huts

This group of Beehive Huts are mostly ruined, although the recreated inside of one hut can be seen. The huts were built by a method called corbelling – no mortar was used and each stone supported the other above it, set in such a way that the rain ran off – giving the look of a beehive. They were used during the dark ages when Ireland was the location of many monasteries. Monks lived and worked in these tiny huts. Charge to see inside of hut, but the remains of the others can be seen easily from the car park.

Food and drink

There are shops and pubs in Ballyferriter and Ventry, and a café just past Slea Head. Refreshments are available at the Blasket Centre and the Celtic and Prehistoric Museum.

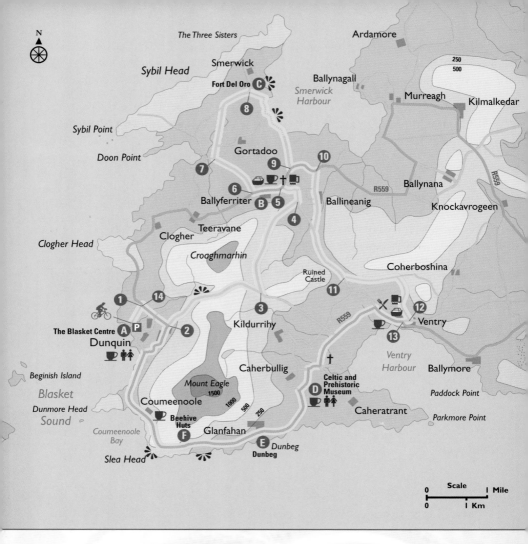

N

The Three Sisters

Ardamore

Sybil Head

Smerwick

Fort Del Oro **C**

Ballynagall

250
500

Smerwick Harbour

Murreagh

Kilmalkedar

Sybil Point

8

Doon Point

7

Gortadoo

9

†

10

R559

Ballynana

Knockavrogeen

6

Ballyferriter **B** **5**

Ballineanig

4

R559

Clogher Head

Clogher

Teeravane

Croaghmarhin

Coherboshina

Ruined Castle

11

1

14

3

Kildurrihy

R559

12

Ventry

The Blasket Centre **A** **P**

2

13

Dunquin

Caherbullig

Ventry Harbour

Ballymore

Beginish Island

Mount Eagle
1500

Paddock Point

Blasket

Dunmore Head

Coumeenoole

1000
500
250

Celtic and Prehistoric Museum **D**

†

Parkmore Point

Sound

Beehive Huts

Glanfahan

Caheratrant

Coumeenoole Bay

F

E Dunbeg
Dunbeg

Slea Head

Scale

0 _____ 1 Mile

0 _____ 1 Km

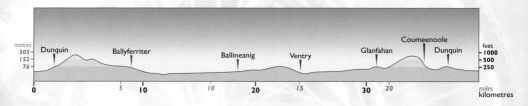

metres
305
152
76

Dunquin

Ballyferriter

Ballineanig

Ventry

Glanfahan

Coumeenoole

Dunquin

feet
1000
500
250

0   5   10   10   20   15   30   20   miles
kilometres

Fort Del Oro

Route description

Start from Blasket Centre car park. Exit to climb hill.

1 TR at TJ opposite An Oige (Youth Hostel), no SP. Descend.

2 TL, SP Ceann Tra/An Daingean. For steep climb then descent – CARE. Opposite fake historical monument on RHS:

3 TL along narrow lane, no SP (5km/3miles). When road bears ninety degrees R:

4 TL along grass centered track, no SP (7.5km/4.5 miles). Enter Ballyferriter (Baile an Fheirtearaigh).

5 TL at TJ, no SP (church on RHS, café and museum opposite). Pass through village.

6 TR, SP Golf Chursa.   **9.5km (6 miles)**

7 TR, SP The Old Barn Gallery. Pass SP yellow walker on LHS.

8 TR at TJ, SP Fort Del Oro. Follow this road all way to beach and TR along beach. Pass concrete groyne and exit into small car park. Continue away from sea.

9 TL at TJ, no SP.   **16.5km (10.5 miles)**

10 TR, SP Ceann Tra/An Daingean, and climb steadily. Just after ruined castle on RHS:

11 TL at XR, SP yellow walker with a crook (other direction SP Rathanane Castle).

12 TR at TJ, no SP. Descend towards sea.   **24km (15 miles)**

13 TR at TJ, no SP. Pass Skipper Restaurant on RHS and continue along beautiful road around Slea Head.

14 TL, SP Heritage Centre, and continue into Dunquin to finish ride.   **40km (25 miles)**

KILLORGLIN AND GLENCAR

Route information

Distance 43.5km (27 miles)

Grade Moderate

Terrain Tarmac surfaces through-out, across gently undulating terrain.

Time to allow 3–5 hours.

Getting there by car Killorglin is on the N72, heading west from Killarney. There is a car park on RHS 50m after direction 1.

Getting there by train There is no practical railway access to this route.

A route for attractive scenery. From Killorglin, the route heads south, gradually climbing a valley with the mighty Macgillycuddy's Reeks becoming increasingly prominent on the left-hand side. A gentle pass takes you past the picturesque Lough Acoose and onto the Climbers Inn. Turning north the route follows an attractive road through yet more lovely scenery and expansive views across Lough Caragh. The route continues along the western shore of the lough, before returning to Killorglin.

Places of interest along the route

A Killorglin

Killorglin is on the Ring of Kerry, which runs around the Iveragh Peninsula. For most of the year Killorglin exists as a pretty village, but during the second week of August a feral goat is brought into town for the Puck Fair. The goat represents Lug, an Irish mythological god, adversary of the one-eyed sun god. This gives the locals and visitors alike a good excuse to fill the pubs and appreciate the music.

B Glencar

Centred in the middle of Ireland's highest peaks, the area around Glencar is extremely attractive. As its name suggests, it has links to Glencoe in Scotland and attracts walkers and climbers who come to enjoy the Macgillycuddy's Reeks to the east and the mountains around Knocknagappie to the west.

Food and drink

There is plenty of choice in Killorglin.

Lake View House, Lough Acoose
Caravan park and B&B serving teas during the summer.

Climbers Inn, Bealalaw Bridge
Drinks and meals served. Outdoor seating.

Rowan Tree, Shanacashel
Traditional pub and shop.

Near Killorglin

N

Castlemaine Harbour

Tullig

Garrane

Clash Island

250

Killorglin

7 1

A

2

N70

N72

River Laune

Cromane

Knockaunaglashy

Illaunstookagh

Lough Yganavan

Farrantoreen Lough

Meanus

Knockaunroe

N70

Caragh Creek

Dooks

Caragh Bridge

6

5

River Caragh

Lough Caragh

Cottoners River

Coppagh Bridge

Lough Nafanida

250

500

Coomcloghaun Lough

Glenbeigh

Seefin
1500

1000

Cummernamuck Lough

Finglass River

Giant's Scar

500

250

Lough Nakirka

500

Cottoners River

Knockbrack

Skregbeg

Lough Nambrackdarrig

Lough Nanoon

Skregmore

Owbeg River

Shanacashel

4

Rowan Tree

1000

Lake View House

Coomloughra Lough

Beenkeragh

Glencar

B

Meelagh River

River Caragh

Caraghbeg River

Climbers Inn

3

Bealalaw Bridge

500

Lough Acoose

Macgillycuddy's

Carrauntoohil

Caher

3000

2500

Reeks

1000

Curraghmore

1500

Lake Curraghmore

Scale

0 — 1 Mile

0 — 1 Km

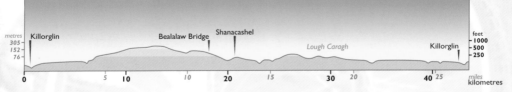

metres
305
152
76

Killorglin

Bealalaw Bridge

Shanacashel

Lough Caragh

Killorglin

feet
1000
500
250

0

5

10

10

20

15

30

20

40

25

miles
kilometres

56

Route description

Start from the bridge across the River Laune. Head uphill into Killorglin.

1 TL at XR, SP Beaufort/Glencar.

2 TR, SP Glencar. Gradually climb.

3 TR, SP Glencar House Hotel.
16.5km (10.5 miles)

4 TL at XR, no SP (shop opposite).

5 RHF, no SP. *33.5km (21 miles)*

6 Shortly, TR at TJ, no SP. Pass large houses in woods on RHS. Bear L following blue arrow. Continue into Killorglin.

7 TR at TJ (roundabout) in centre of Killorglin to finish the ride. *43.5km (27 miles)*

Lough Acoose

Route 14

KILGARVAN AND LOUGH ATOOREEN

Route information

Distance 45.5km (28.5 miles)

Grade Strenuous

Terrain Four long climbs. The route follows back roads that are rough in places.

Time to allow 5–7 hours.

Getting there by car Kilgarvan is on the R569 east of Kenmare. There is on-street parking.

Getting there by train There is no practical railway access to this route.

Starting in Kilgarvan the route heads briefly along the R569 before it starts the first climb of the day, passing the highest pub in Ireland. A traverse with far reaching views leads to a descent into Ballingeary before the second and easiest climb over the pass of Keimaneigh. Just before Kealkill, the shortest but steepest of the climbs leads past the picturesque Lough Atooreen. The final climb is around the edge of a bowl shaped valley with far-reaching views.

The reward is a descent practically all the way back to Kilgarvan, where in places the road hugs the side of the mountain.

Places of interest along the route

A Kilgarvan Motor Museum, near Kilgarvan

Developed from a private collection, the motor museum is tucked away in three sheds on the side of the hill. Approximately 30 cars are on view, from Rolls Royces to a Beetle Cabriolet. There is a pleasant informal feel about the place with none of the vehicles roped off. All the cars start and are still run out at fairs and weddings. Small, basic tearoom. Open all year, daily 0930–1800. Charge.

Food and drink

Kilgarvan and Ballingeary have shops and pubs. Several cafés and shops are passed en route.

Top of Coom, near Kilgarvan
The highest pub in Ireland. Outdoor seating, although no real views.

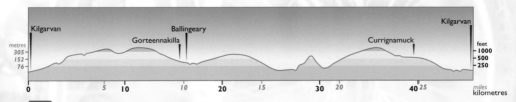

Elevation profile: Kilgarvan, Gorteennakilla, Ballingeary, Currignamuck, Kilgarvan. metres 305 / 152 / 76; feet 1000 / 500 / 250. Scale in miles and kilometres: 0, 5, 10, 15, 20, 25, 30, 40.

Shrine, Kilgarvan

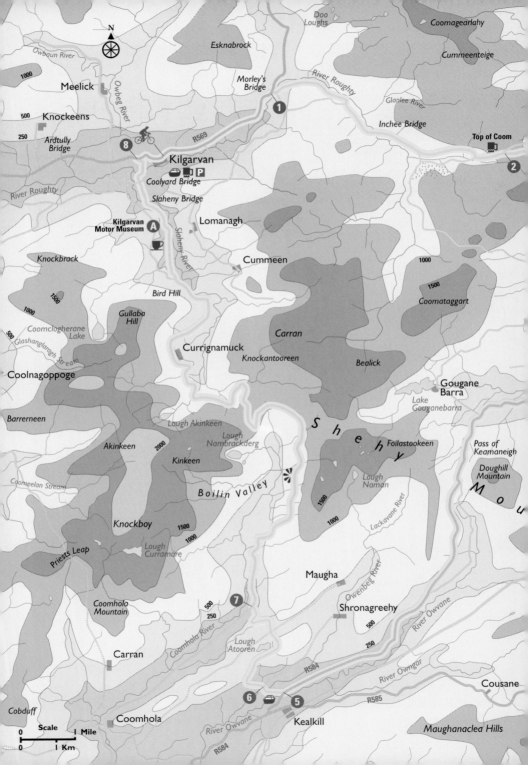

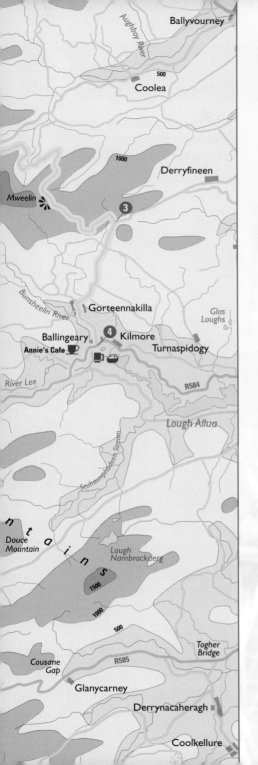

Start opposite the village grill, with Jack Healy Rae behind. Head L and slightly uphill.

1   TR, SP Ballingeary/Gougane Barra. Cross River Roughty.

2   TR, SP Gougane Barra.

13.5km (8.5 miles)

3   TR at TJ, SP Beal Atha/An Ghaorhaigh/ Gougane Barra (22.5km/14 miles). Descend and enter Ballingeary.

4   TR at TJ, SP Bantry/Glengarriff (famine pot on LHS). Just before crossing bridge, in front of castle and statue:

5   TR, no SP.

6   LHF, no SP, for hard climb.

45.5km (28.5 miles)

7   TR at TJ, no SP but junction box on telegraph pole on RHS (50.5km/31.5 miles). Continue towards Kilgarvan, passing motor museum.

8   TR at TJ, SP Killarney/Macroom, and into Kilgarvan to finish ride.

45.5km (28.5 miles)

15

CASTLETOWN BERE AND ALLIHIES

Route information

Distance 49km (30.5 miles)

Grade Strenuous

Terrain The roads are generally well-surfaced except for a section out of Castletown Bere which is pitted in places. There is a steady climb out of Castletown Bere and numerous short but steep ascents and descents north of Allihies.

Time to allow 4–6 hours.

Getting there by car Castletown Bere is on the west side of the Beara Peninsula, on the R572. There is car parking by the harbour.

Getting there by train There is no practical railway access to this route.

Starting from Castletown Bere, the ride heads west and inland, climbing past two interesting archeological sites (good views back the way). Dropping back to the R572, the route follows two passes, the second affording a lovely view across Allihies (better if the sea is rough). Passing through Allihies, the route rises and falls around the Slieve Miskish Mountains, offering excellent sea vistas along the way. It is worth taking the brief side trip to check out the colourful village of Eyeries before the final low pass back into Castletown Bere.

Places of interest along the route

A Castletown Bere

Castletown Bere lies next to the world's second largest natural harbour and for this reason is primarily a fishing port. The town originally grew up in the 19th century, with the discovery of copper around Allihies. Today Castletown Bere is the largest town on the Beara Peninsula. There is a small museum in the old schoolhouse. Contact the Tourist Office for more information on (027) 70054.

B Derrintaggart West Stone Circle

Lying in view of Miskisk Mountain, Derrintaggart West Stone Circle is one of six stone circles on the Beara Peninsula. There were once 15 stones (typical of the other circles where there are between 15 and 19 stones), but three have fallen. There is also a cooking area, where hot stones were rolled into water to boil it and cook meat such as deer and goat. Free access although a donation for charity is appreciated. Signposted from the route.

C Teernahillane Ring Fort

Looking like a large flat scone in the middle of a field, Teernahillane Ring Fort is worth a walk although, apart from the sides where pallets have been tied in an attempt to preserve the fort's shape, there is little to see bar the grazing sheep. Free access. Signposted just off the route.

D Dursey Island

Connected to the mainland by cable car, Dursey Island is 607ha (1,500 acres) of rugged terrain and pasture land. Today the island is home to fewer than a dozen people. The signal tower provides a point of interest. Ireland's only cable car runs daily, Monday–Saturday 0900–2000, Sunday four crossings to coincide with church services.

Ⓔ Allihies

At one time, following the discovery of copper in 1810, 1300 people worked around Allihies. Today the remains of cottages lived in by Cornishmen and fenced off mineshafts are the legacy of this period. Tourism is the dominant industry today and the village has a good beach.

Route description

Start from harbour (opposite supermarket) and head through town following SP Allihies/ Dursey.

1   TR, SP Derrintaggart Stone Circle. Then TL, SP Derrintaggart Stone Circle. Climb, passing stone circle and then ring fort on RHS.

---

2   TR at TJ, no SP, for steady climb over one pass, then a climb over the Bealbarnish Gap. Follow road towards Allihies. You will pass TL for Dursey Island.

Castletown Bere Haven

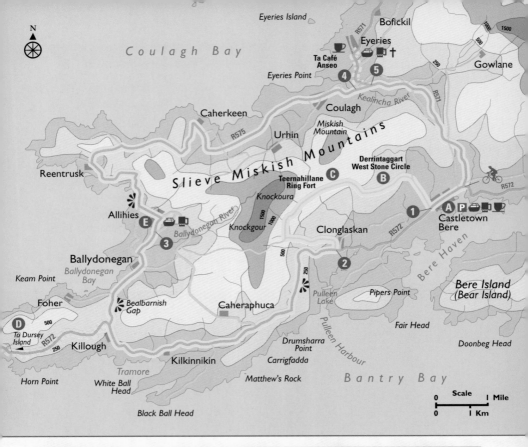

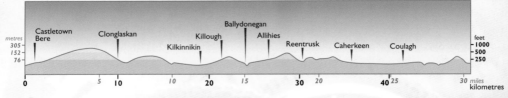

3 TL, SP Allihies (25.5km/16 miles). Cycle through village and follow SP Ring of Beara. Continue towards Eyeries.

4 To visit Eyeries, TL.

Otherwise, TR, SP Castletown Bere.

41km (25.5 miles)

5 TR at TJ, SP Castletown Bere. Follow road into Castletown Bere to finish the ride by the harbour. **49km (30.5 miles)**

Food and drink

There are shops and pubs in Castletown Bere, Allihies and Eyeries.

Ta Café Anseo, Eyeries
Café with seating in what feels like someone's living room.

16 CAHIR AND CLOGHEEN

Route information

Distance 53km (33 miles)

Grade Easy

Terrain Mostly quiet lanes. There are a few hills to climb.

Time to allow 4–6 hours.

Getting there by car Cahir is on the N24 Clonmel/Tipperary road. There is a pay and display car park between the castle and the Tourist Office.

Getting there by train There is a railway station at Cahir. For travel information telephone (1850) 36622 or visit www.irishrail.ie

From Cahir, the route heads south, past the entrance to Swiss Cottage, to the village of Ardfinnan. There are lovely views as you approach and then climb out of the village before heading west to Clogheen. If you are feeling energetic, a trip along the R668 into the Knockmealdown Mountains is worth the effort for the expansive views – follow the R668 for approximately 4km (2.5 miles) as far as The Vee, a well-known viewpoint. The main route follows back lanes, giving an opportunity to visit Mitchelstown Caves before returning to Cahir. Contact Cahir Tourist Office on (052) 41453 for more information on the area.

Route description

Start at car park between castle and Tourist Office. Leave car park to TR at TJ, no SP (opposite Castle Arms). Pass Tourist Office on RHS.

1 TR along R670, SP Ardfinnan. Pass Swiss Cottage and continue into Ardfinnan.

2 TR at TJ, SP Clogheen. **9km (5.5 miles)**

3 TL, SP Goatenbridge.

4 TL, SP Suir Drive/Kilmaneen.

5 TR at XR, SP Clogheen.

6 TL at TJ, no SP (14.5km/9 miles). Pass community alert SP on LHS. Enter Goatenbridge.

7 TR at TJ, SP Clogheen. Continue towards Clogheen.

8 For a trip into the Knockmealdown Mountains, TL at TJ.

Otherwise, TR at TJ, SP Clogheen (25km/ 15.5 miles). Enter Clogheen.

9 TL at TJ, SP Ballyporeen/Mitchelstown.

10 TR at XR, SP Burncourt.

11 SO at XR (29.5km/18.5 miles) along tree-lined avenue, no SP.

12 TR at TJ, SP Burncourt.

13 TL, SP Mitchelstown Caves (34.5km/ 21.5 miles). Pass caves.

14 TR at TJ, SP Burncourt. Enter Burncourt.

15 TL at TJ, SP Cahir (43km/27 miles). Continue towards Cahir.

16 TL at TJ, no SP.

17 TR at TJ, SP Town Centre, and finish the ride at the car park. **53km (33 miles)**

Places of interest along the route

Ⓐ Cahir

Dominating the centre of Cahir is the castle. Founded in 1142, it is in remarkably good condition because its occupants surrendered to Cromwell in 1650. There were also two periods of extensive restoration during the 19th and 20th centuries. Sitting on a rocky island in the River Suir, the castle has a working portcullis, massive walls and towers. A number of exhibitions explain other aspects of local history. Duchas property. Open all year, daily 1000–1600 (summer closes 1900). Charge. Telephone (052) 41011; www.heritageireland.ie.

Ⓑ Swiss Cottage, near Cahir

Recently restored, Swiss Cottage was designed by the architect John Nash as a retreat for the local nobles. It is designed to look entirely natural, as if it had grown from the ground. Duchas property. Open May to September, daily 1000–1800. Charge. Telephone (052) 41011; www.heritageireland.ie

Ⓒ Church, near Clogheen

The ruined church to the west of Clogheen has a *Sheela na gig* on its wall. Generally only seen in museums, these are rarely found in situ. They are solitary carvings of naked female forms and each one is different. There are many theories as to their significance – one explanation is that they were a morality lesson for the illiterate faithful. Other theories say that they were to repel evil or were involved in healing. Free access at all reasonable times.

Knockastakeen

Sturrakeen

N

Galty Mountains

Farbreaga

Lough Muskry

Greenane

2000

1500

Boolakennedy
Glengara

Glengara Wood

N8

Burncourt

14

D

Mitchelstown Caves

13 Coolantallagh

Lisfunshion

11

12

Ballyporeen

R665

River Duag

Glenacunna

N24

N8

A

R670

17

Cahir

N24

1

N24

Derrygrath

Ballymacadam

16

Ballindoney

Swiss
Cottage

B

Clonmore

River Suir

N8

R670

500

250

Kilcommon

R668

15

Monroe

Ballylooby

Thonoge River

R665

Ardfinnan

3

2

Ballytrehy

4

Hylands

6

Ballyveera

Castlegrace

5

Ballyboy

R665

Ballyknockane

Clogheen

9

Bohernagore

10

C

Church

8

River Tar

7

Goatenbridge

250

250

500

1000

250

R668

The Vee

500

1000

Roches
Hill

Scale

0 | Mile

1500

Knockshanahullion

Sugarloaf Hill

1500

Crohan West

0   1 Km

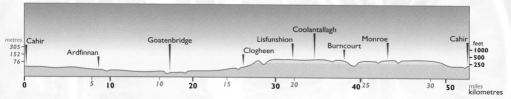

metres   Cahir   Coolantallagh   Cahir   feet
305   Goatenbridge   Lisfunshion   Monroe   1000
152   Ardfinnan   Clogheen   Burncourt   500
76   250

0   5   10   15   20   25   30   miles
0   10   20   30   40   50   kilometres

D Mitchelstown Caves, near Mitchelstown

Discovered in 1833 when Michael Condon dropped his crowbar down a crevasse, Mitchelstown Caves are still in the same family ownership – the Mulcahys who bought the farm in 1875. There is 1km (0.6 mile) of caves, naturally created in the limestone. Features include massive caverns, calcite columns and fossils. Largely uncommercialized, visitors buy tickets from the farmhouse. Open all year, daily 1000–1800. Charge. Telephone (052) 67246.

Food and drink

Pubs and shops in Cahir, Ardfinnan and Burncourt. There is a shop in Goatenbridge and a prettily painted rural pub is passed between Goatenbridge and Clogheen.

Pub, Cahir

TIPPERARY AND GALBALLY

Route information

Distance   53km (33 miles)

Grade   Moderate

Terrain   Good roads throughout. There is a well-graded, steady climb out of Tipperary.

Time to allow   4–6 hours.

Getting there by car   Tipperary is on the N74. There is on-street parking.

Getting there by train   There is a railway station at Tipperary (a single, small platform). For travel information telephone (1850) 366222 or visit www.irishrail.ie

From Tipperary the route heads south, climbing through woods to the Glen of Aherlow and expansive views across the Galty Mountains. A descent follows a pretty valley to the village of Galbally. From there, the second half of the route involves a glorious ride back through the Glen of Aherlow, with the Galty Mountains prominent on the right hand side. A visit to a child's graveyard shouldn't be missed before returning to Tipperary along a series of quiet lanes.

Places of interest along the route

Ⓐ Tipperary

Famous from the marching song written in 1912, Tipperary is a quiet market town. It was one of the centres of the Civil War in the early 20th century and there is a small museum at the swimming pool exhibiting memorabilia from between 1919 and 1923. Open all year, Monday–Saturday 0930–1700. Contact the Tourist Office on (062) 51457.

Ⓑ Glen of Aherlow

Overlooking the Galty Mountains, the Glen of Aherlow is an attractive place to stop and admire the view. The Galties themselves are the highest mountain range in Ireland and an excellent view is afforded from the pull in by the side of the road. Overlooking all of this is a tall statue of Christ the King. Erected in 1950 and then re-erected 25 years later, it blesses the glen, its people and those who pass by.

Ⓒ Moor Abbey, near Galbally

Founded by Donough O'Brien in the 13th century, Moor Abbey is an attractive ruin close to the road. Its history is rather bloody – it was plundered in 1472, suppressed in 1540 and its friars massacred in 1570. Today the building comprises a small roofless ruin, which can be easily explored. Picnic tables. Free access at all reasonable times.

Ⓓ Child's Graveyard, Ardane

A poignant place to visit. Many years ago, if a child was not baptized before dying, he or she could not be buried on consecrated ground. As a result, these children were buried here. Originally, each tiny grave was marked by a small gravestone, but at some time these have been gathered up to form an enclosure in the shadow of the neighbouring trees.

Route description

Start from the railway station. Exit to TR at TJ, no SP. Cross railway.

1 TR at mini roundabout, SP Golf Chumann/ Tipperary Golf Club. Pass golf club on LHS. Climb steadily through woods.

2 TR at TJ along R663, SP Lisvarrinane/ Galbally. **9km (5.5 miles)**

3 TL at TJ, SP Mitchelstown.
19km (12 miles)

4 TL at XR, SP Anglesboro.

5 Take RHF, no SP. Cross stone bridge.

6 To visit the child's graveyard, TR and pass two bungalows on LHS. Continue along track. Walk through first gate on LHS, pass straight through field to a gap in hedge and through next field to a small wood. The graveyard is in the wood.

Otherwise, TL at XR, no SP (but back the way SP Eatharlach/Glen of Aherlow).
39.5km (24.5 miles)

7 Bear R at XR (follow road around to R as two roads come in from L), no SP.

8 TL opposite farm buildings, no SP.

9 TL at TJ, no SP (bridge RHS).

10 TR opposite garage, no SP. Cross stone bridge.

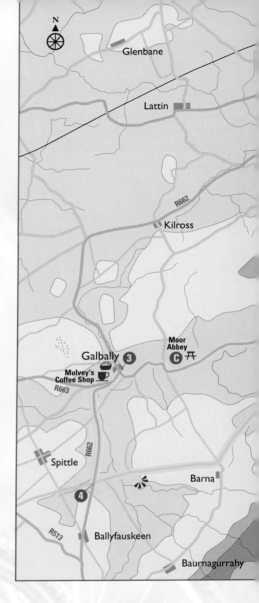

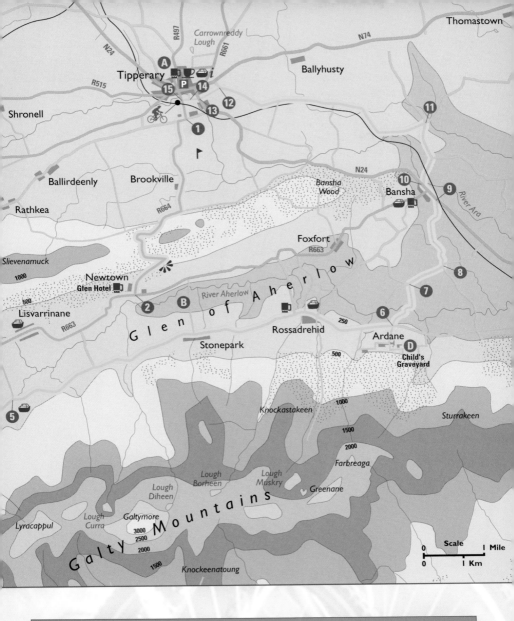

Thomastown

R497

Carrownreddy Lough

N74

R661

A

Tipperary

Ballyhusty

R515

P

15   **14**   **i**

11

13   **12**

Shronell

1

Ballirdeenly

Brookville

N24

Bansha Wood

10

Bansha

9

River Ara

Rathkea

R664

Foxfort

R663

Slievenamuck

1000

8

Newtown

Glen Hotel

River Aherlow

Glen of Aherlow

7

500

2   **B**

6

Lisvarrinane

R663

Rossadrehid

250

5

Stonepark

500

Ardane

D

Child's Graveyard

Knockastakeen

1000

Sturrakeen

1500

2000

Farbreaga

Lough Borheen

Lough Muskry

Greenane

Lough Diheen

Galty Mountains

Lough Curra

Galtymore

3000

2500

Lyracappul

2000

1500

Knockeenatoung

Scale

0 _____ 1 Mile

0 _____ 1 Km

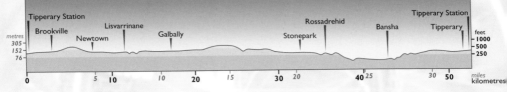

metres
305
152
76

Tipperary Station
Brookville
Newtown
Lisvarrinane
Galbally
Stonepark
Rossadrehid
Bansha
Tipperary Station
Tipperary

feet
1000
500
250

0   5   10   15   20   25   30   50

miles
kilometres

11 TL at XR along lane parallel to railway, no SP but next to Kilfeade community alert SP.

46.5km (29 miles)

12 SO at roundabout, no SP (white bollards either side), later pass fire station on LHS.

13 SO at XR, no SP (raised triangular grass area opposite). Cross N24 (CARE).

14 TL at TJ, no SP.

15 TL at TJ opposite hotel, no SP. Return to railway station to finish the ride.

53km (33 miles)

Food and drink

Plenty of choice in Tipperary. Lisvarrinane has a shop and there are shops and pubs in Galbally, Rossadrehid and Bansha.

The Seamrog, Tipperary
Serves all day breakfasts and sandwiches.

Glen Hotel, Newtown
Meals available. Outdoor seating.

Child's Graveyard, Ardane

THE DINGLE PENINSULA

Route information

Distance   59.5km (37 miles)

Grade   Moderate

Terrain   Mostly well graded roads throughout the route. There is one small climb towards the end of the route.

Time to allow   5–7 hours.

Getting there by car   Dingle, on the N86, is the major town on the Dingle peninsula. There is a car park by the harbour.

Getting there by train   There is no practical railway access to this route.

From the attractive town of Dingle the route heads west through Ventry towards Slea Head. The road hugs the coast and you are faced with glorious sea views to the left and a variety of historical attractions on the landward side, including forts, beehive huts and a restored famine house. On through Dunquin, you are treated to more wonderful views on the way to Ballyferriter. Cycling more inland now, the route passes the perfectly preserved oratory at Gallarus before returning towards the coast again. The remainder of the ride is inland, initially under the shadow of Brandon Mountain. The detour to scenic Brandon Cove should not be missed before a final climb over a low pass on the way back to Dingle.

Places of interest along the route

Ⓐ Dingle

Brought to recent prominence by Fungie the dolphin, Dingle is an attractive town with much more to offer. The harbour is a natural focal point and pleasure boats share the water with larger fishing vessels. A large tourist office has been built and pleasure trips into the bay to see the resident solitary bottlenose dolphin can be taken. Opposite the harbour is **Dingle Oceanworld**. This nicely concentrates on local species, including conger eels, giant crayfish and sharks. There is a touch pool and a walk through tunnel. Café. Open all year, daily 0930–1730 (July and August closes 2000). Telephone (066) 9152111. The Tourist Office can be contacted on (066) 9151183.

Ⓑ Celtic and Prehistoric Museum, near Dunquin

With a good degree of comic touch the large guide to the Celtic and Prehistoric Museum leads you through the centuries from Palaeolithic times, through the Bronze Age to Celtic times. See Route 12 for more information.

Ⓒ Dunbeg

The ancient promontory fort at Dunbeg is well preserved. See Route 12 for more information.

Ⓓ Ballyferriter

Named after the Ferriter family whose son Piaras fought in the rebellion of 1642. See Route 12 for more information.

Ⓔ Gallarus Oratory

Built in the late 7th century, Gallarus Oratory is the only fully standing oratory in Ireland.

Shaped like an upturned boat, its only blemish is a slight sag to the roof. There is a single door and window and two stone projections on the inside of the doorway that may have held lighting. Remarkably, no mortar was used in the construction. There were other buildings of the same type in the area – in fact, there is another collapsed example only a few fields away. Café. Charge. Contact Dingle Tourist Office for details of opening times.

Brandon Creek

Long before Christopher Columbus, St Brandon set sail from scenic Brandon Creek in circa 535AD bound for America. Sailing with 14 other monks, it took him seven years to reach America – the story was recounted in a medieval manuscript, the *Navigatio Sancti Brendani*. In 1976, an Oxford graduate repeated the journey, this time taking 13 months via the Hebrides, Faroes, Iceland, Greenland and Newfoundland.

Route description

Start from the Tourist Office and head out of town, passing harbour on LHS.

1 TL at XR (roundabout), SP Slea Head Drive (1km/0.6 miles). Cycle through and follow road around coast towards Ballyferriter – expansive sea and cliff views.

2 TL, SP An Mhuirioch/Gallarus Oratory/Inscribed Stone/Slea Head Drive (34.5km/21.5 miles). Pass Gallarus Oratory. Enter Mhuirioch.

3 TL, SP Begley's on the Pier. Pass tarmac basketball court on RHS, sea on LHS. Just after passing post office on RHS:

4 TR next to Ballynagall, no SP. Pass telephone box on RHS.

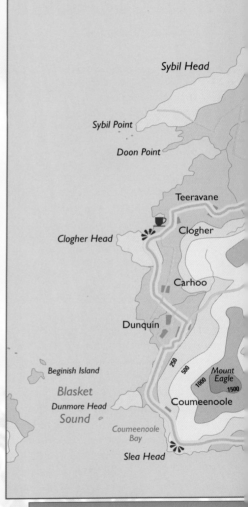

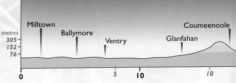

Brandon Creek **F**

Tiduff

Ballydavid Head

Ballyroe

Ballynabuck

River Feohanagh

Brandon
Mountain

2500

6

Feohanagh

Brandon
Peak

*The
Three
Sisters*

Carrigbrean

5

Ardamore

7

Ballinloghig

Gearhane 2000

1500

Smerwick

4

Ballynagall

Mhuirioch

Kilmalkedar

Glin

Lough Namna

Lough Gal

*Smerwick
Harbour*

3

Gallarus

E **Gallarus
Oratory**

Ballysitteragh

Gortadoo

R559

Ballynana

1500

1000

Ballineanig

2

Knockavrogeen

500

D

Ballyferriter

R559

Ballyeightragh

8

500

Lateevebeg

500

250

Knocknahoran

250

Ballybowler

Coherboshina

Milltown

9

Dingle

Kildurrihy

R559

Ventry

1 *i*

A

N86

*Dingle
Harbour*

Caherbullig

*Ventry
Harbour*

Ballymore

Reenbeg

Glanfahan

B **Celtic and
Prehistoric
Museum**

Caheratrant

Paddock Point

250

500

*Reenbeg
Point*

C

Dunbeg

Parkmore Point

Scale
0   1 Mile
0   1 Km

feet
1000
500
250

Dunquin   Clogher   Teeravane   Ballynagall   Feohanagh   Ballynabuck   Dingle
                              Ballyferriter   Ballyroe   Knocknahoran

20   15   30   20   40 25   30   50   35

miles
kilometres

5   TL at TJ, no SP (41km/25.5 miles). Follow road as it descends gently towards sea.

6   TL, SP Slea Head Drive/Bandon Creek.

7   TL at TJ, SP An Daingean/Slea Head Drive (48km/30 miles). Continue towards Dingle.

8   TL along grass centred road, no SP (Ballyhea Fisheries opposite).

56km (35 miles)

9   TL at TJ, no SP. Pass 30 km/h SP. Follow this road through one-way system to TR at roundabout. Return to Tourist Office to finish ride.   *59.5km (37 miles)*

Food and drink

There are pubs and cafés in Dingle and Ventry. Ballyferriter has a shop and Ballynagall a pub.

Dingle

KILLARNEY AND GAP OF DUNLOE

Route information

Distance 59.5km (37 miles)

Grade Strenuous

Terrain Two hard climbs and one short section of path that can be walked. The roads through the Muckross estate are good quality.

Time to allow 4–7 hours.

Getting there by car Killarney is south of Tralee on the N22. There is a long stay pay and display car park next to the Tourist Office, the start of the route.

Getting there by train There is a railway station in Killarney. For travel information telephone (1850) 366222 or visit www.irishrail.ie

This ride is best started early as the picturesque Gap of Dunloe is usually busy with tourist traffic. From Killarney a steady climb takes you over the Gap of Dunloe for a descent into the Black Valley. The route then follows the Owenreagh River upstream, for a strenuous climb to Moll's Gap, on the Ring of Kerry. There are plenty of good views and you descend to the Muckross estate, passing Ladies View (views across the Killarney lakes). The final section of the route uses busy roads and jaunting tracks to return to Killarney.

Places of interest along the route

A Killarney

One of the most visited towns in Ireland. **St Mary's Cathedral** was used as a hospice during the famine and a tree in front of the cathedral marks the spot where the victims were buried. If you wish to see vintage bicycles then the **Museum of Irish Transport** is the place to visit. There are also cars and fire engines and an 1844 Meteor Stanley tricycle, unused because the shop that stocked it never sold it! Open April to October, daily 1000–1800 (July and August closes 2000). Charge. Contact the Tourist Office on (064) 31633.

B Gap of Dunloe

Notoriously busy, though with due reason as it is quite beautiful, the Gap of Dunloe sees many visitors. It was carved by glacial melt waters and the narrow road is liable to be packed with jaunting cars (pony traps) taking visitors up and over the gap. For these reasons it is best visited early in the day, when even in summer you may have the place to yourself. Free access.

C Muckross Estate

Built in 1843, Muckross House was considered grand enough for Queen Victoria when she visited Killarney. The house and its 4452ha (11,000 acres) were donated to the nation in 1932. The house is open to visitors and contains exhibits principally from the 19th century. Open all year, daily 0900–1800 (closes later in July and August, earlier in winter). Surrounding the house are beautiful gardens, laid out by Arthur

Bourn Vincent. They contain a huge variety of plants, as the soil is a mix of acid and alkali. Nearby and signposted is the impressive Torc Waterfall. On the estate there is also a tearoom, craft centre and working farm. Open all year, daily. Telephone (064) 31440; www.muckross-house.ie

D Muckross Friary

Founded in 1448, there are extensive remains of this fine Irish gothic building. The choir and nave date from the 15th century whilst the central tower and south transept date from the 16th century. All four of Kerry's great Gaelic poets are buried here. Three are within the walls whilst Piaras Feiftear, who was hung in Killarney, is buried somewhere in the grounds. Free access at all reasonable times.

Route description

Start from Killarney Tourist Office. Head out of town, passing car park on RHS.

1 TR at TJ, SP Ring of Kerry.

2 TL at roundabout, SP Killorglin/Dingle/Ring of Kerry.

3 TL, SP Gap of Dunloe. **6.5km (4 miles)**

4 TL, SP Gap of Dunloe. At entrance continue through car park and up the Gap of Dunloe.

5 LHF, SP Kenmare.

6 RHF, no SP (other direction SP Brandon's Cottage). **22.5km (14 miles)**

7 LHF, SP Killarney for hard zig-zag climb.

8 TL at TJ, SP Kenmare/Killarney. **32km (20 miles)**

9 TL at TJ, SP Killarney. Descend, next turn is easy to miss, SO; 1 km (0.6 miles) after passing SP Killarney National Park:

10 TL onto narrow white path running next to road (50.5km/31.5 miles), SP Muckross House and Gardens/Torc Waterfall. Pass small wooded car park on RHS. Follow path as it bears L with wooden fence in front. Descend and cross stream.

11 TL at TJ, SP Muckross House and Gardens. Follow this tarmac road through gardens to see Muckross House on RHS. Follow road as it bears 90 degrees R, to head for L of house. Level with house, head 90 degrees L and cycle away from house along a road used by jaunting cars. SO at next XR to see Lough Leane on LHS. At next junction bear L. When road meets N71:

12 TL at TJ, no SP (54.5km/34 miles). You can use jaunting car track on LHS of N71 for much of the way. Later, follow SP Town Centre.

13 TL, SP Knockreer/Tourist Office and finish the ride. **59.5km (37 miles)**

Food and drink

Plenty of choice in Killarney. Three cafés are passed along the route.

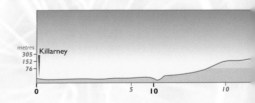

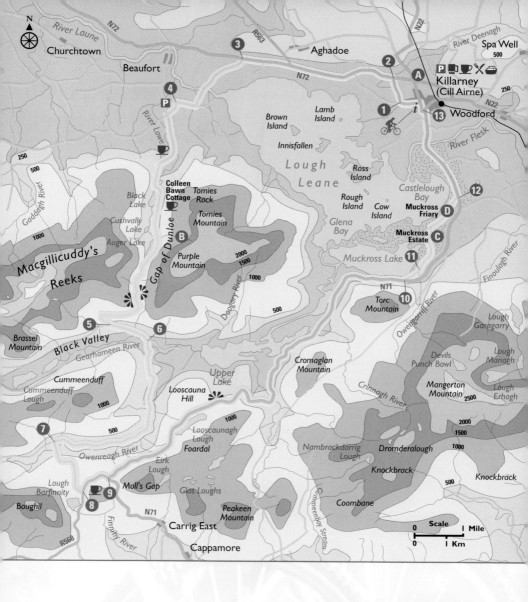

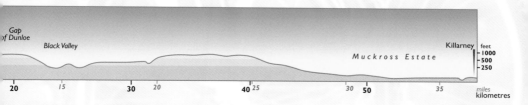

WATERVILLE AND VALENCIA ISLAND

Route information

🚴 **Distance** 63.5km (39.5 miles)

🚴 **Grade** Strenuous

🚴 **Terrain** Generally well-surfaced roads over gently undulating terrain. One hard climb.

🚴 **Time to allow** 4–7 hours.

🚴 **Getting there by car** Waterville, on the N70, is on the Ring of Kerry. There is plenty of on-street parking.

🚴 **Getting there by train** There is no practical railway access to this route.

Starting from Waterville, the route heads around the Skellig Ring (the Skelligs are islands off Valencia). After a short distance along the N70, the roads are quiet as tourist coaches are discouraged all the way to the beach at Ballinskelligs. The next section of the route is hard (with the reward of fabulous views), with a climb over a mountain pass before descending into Portmagee. Onto Valencia Island, via a bridge, and around the southern coast, before taking a ferry from Knightstown back to the mainland. Back roads lead into Cahersiveen, before returning to Waterville along the N70. For more information on the area, contact Cahersiveen Tourist Office on (066) 72777.

Places of interest along the route

A Waterville
Overlooking Ballinskelligs Bay, this town is stretched along the seafront. Its claim to fame are visits by Charlie Chaplin and a statue has been erected in his memory.

B Ballinskelligs
With a beautiful outlook and a sandy beach, Ballinskelligs is a good place to stop. Boat trips to the Skellig Islands are available from here. Across a narrow inlet, easily forded, is a tower house built by the MacCarthys (easy to reach and climb). The town is at the centre of the Kerry Gaeltacht, Kerry's Gaelic speaking area..

C Megalithic Tomb
Easily accessible in a field just off the road. Free access.

D The Skellig Experience, Valencia Island
This visitor centre describes the history of the two Skellig islands. Situated 12.5km (8 miles) off the coast, Skellig Michael and Little Skellig have a varied history. Between the 7th and 13th centuries, there was an active monastery on Skellig Michael and there are still reasonably substantial remains, including two oratories and six beehive huts. The lighthouse was automated in 1986 but has provided over 150 years of service. Today birds are the chief inhabitants of the islands, with over 20,000 breeding pairs of gannets on Little Skellig. The visitor centre has its own boat and offers boat trips to the islands themselves (although, unlike other trips, they do not land on Skellig Michael). Open May to September, daily 1000–1800. Charge.

Ballinskelligs Bay

Ⓔ Valencia Island

Connected to the mainland by a bridge and a ferry, Valencia Island has an illustrious past. In 1858 a transatlantic cable was laid from here to America to allow direct communication. Messages were sent by morse code and by World War I over 200 men were employed here. They enjoyed an excellent lifestyle and evidence of their grand housing is seen at Knightstown, the main village on the island. A museum in Knightstown's old school reveals the local history.

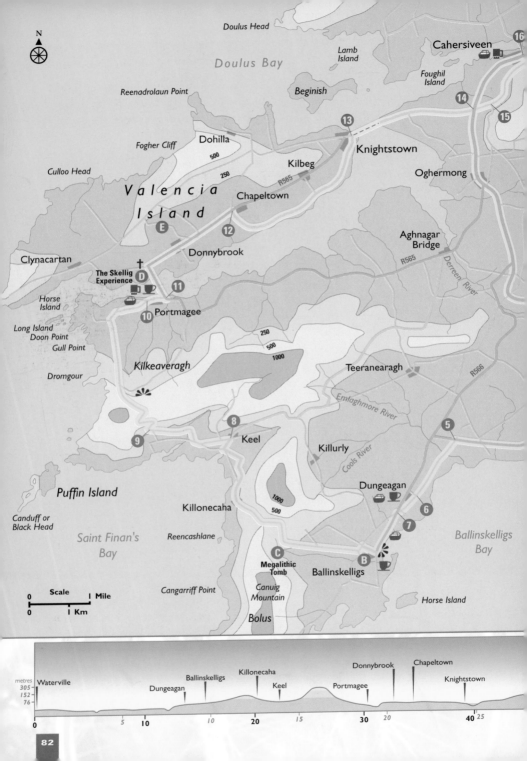

N

Doulus Head

Doulus Bay

Lamb
Island

Cahersiveen

16

Reenadrolaun Point

Beginish

Foughil
Island

14

15

Fogher Cliff

Dohilla

500

Kilbeg

13

Knightstown

Oghermong

Culloo Head

250

R565

Chapeltown

Valencia
Island

E

12

Donnybrook

Aghnagar
Bridge

R565

Derreen River

Clynacartan

The Skellig
Experience

D

11

Horse
Island

10

Portmagee

Long Island
Doon Point
Gull Point

250

500

1000

Teeranearagh

R566

Dromgour

Kilkeaveragh

Emlaghmore River

Cools River

8

5

9

Keel

Killurly

Puffin Island

Dungeagan

6

Canduff or
Black Head

Killonecaha

1000

7

Ballinskelligs
Bay

Saint Finan's
Bay

Reencashlane

500

Cangarriff Point

C

Megalithic
Tomb

Canuig
Mountain

B

Ballinskelligs

Horse Island

Bolus

Scale
0   1 Mile
0   1 Km

metres
305
152
76

Waterville

Dungeagan

Ballinskelligs

Killonecaha

Donnybrook

Chapeltown

Keel

Portmagee

Knightstown

0   5   10   10   20   15   30   20   40 25

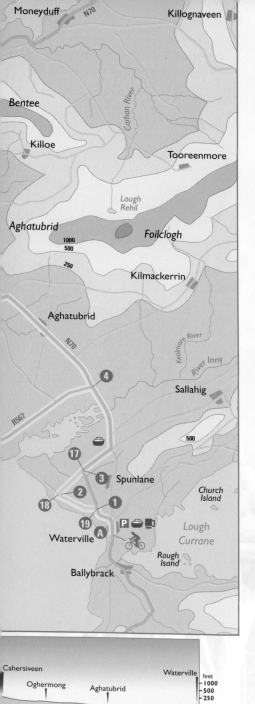

Route description

Start by the Charlie Chaplin statue, opposite Bay View Hotel. Head L, with sea on LHS, and bear L opposite Gaelic cross, SP Tralee/ Cahersiveen.

1 TL along coast road, SP Smugglers Inn.

2 TR, crown SP (grass centred track opposite junction).

3 TL at TJ along centrally lined road, crown SP.

4 TL, SP Ballinskelligs. **5.5km (3.5 miles)**

5 TL, crown SP.

6 TL at TJ (effectively SO), no SP.

7 TL at TJ, SP B an Sceilg (13.5km/8.5 miles). Continue through Ballinskelligs and follow road towards Portmagee.

8 TL at TJ, SP Portmagee, for hard climb.

9 Bear R, SP Portmagee (25.5km/16 miles). Hard climb continues.

10 TR at TJ, SP Valencia Island.

11 TL, SP Valencia Island (32km/20 miles). Cross bridge, bear R passing Skellig Experience and just before church on LHS:

12 TR along Shore Road, no SP.

13 TR onto ferry, no SP (41km/25.5 miles). After crossing, continue SO.

14 SO at XR, no SP. Cross N70 (CARE).

15 TL at TJ, no SP. Pass 30km/h SP.

16 TL at XR along West Main Street, no SP (45.5km/28.5 miles). Continue towards Waterville.   *45.5km (28.5 miles)*

17 TR, SP Waterville/Golf Links.
60km (37.5 miles)

18 TL at TJ, no SP (parallel to sea).

19 TR at TJ, no SP, and finish the ride by Charlie Chaplin's statue.   *63.5km (39.5 miles)*

View of Portmagee

Food and drink

Waterville, Portmagee and Cahersiveen have shops and pubs. Various shops and pubs are passed along the route. The café/gallery just before Ballinskelligs was considered overpriced and under-portioned by the cyclist who compiled this route. Ballinskelligs itself has a beach shop and café close to beach.

Chocolate Shop, near Portmagee
Chocolates are hand made on the premises for export and local consumption. Free tastings!

BANDON AND CLONAKILTY

Route information

Distance 77km (48 miles)

Grade Moderate

Terrain Good roads throughout.
Most of the route follows the coast
and estuary which is reasonably
flat, with just a couple of climbs
inland.

Time to allow 5–8 hours.

Getting there by car Bandon is
south west of Cork on the N71. There
are several car parks and on-street
parking.

Getting there by train There is
no practical railway access to this
route.

*From Bandon the route heads south along quiet
back lanes through the outskirts of Kilbrittain.
From here the route follows the edge of
attractive Coolmain Bay, passing close to the
magnificent ruined abbey at Timoleague. A few
climbs are involved through the back roads
before you regain estuary views and reach the
attractive town of Clonakilty. The return to
Bandon follows more quiet back lanes.*

Route description

Start from the Tourist Office in Brandon. Head
towards town centre and methodist church.

1 TL at TJ, SP Skibbereen/Clonakilty. At first
junction, TR at XR, no SP. Pass shops either
side. TL at XR along one-way street, SP
Skibbereen. TL at TJ (effectively SO), no SP
(fountain on RHS).

2 TL, SP Kilbrittain.

3 TL at five-way junction, no SP (O'Leary
pub on LHS). Gently climb.

4 TR, no SP but telegraph poles on RHS of
road cross to LHS. ***8km (5 miles)***

5 SO at XR, no SP. Continue downhill.

6 TL at TJ (effectively SO), no SP but
Millennium sundial on LHS.

7 TR, SP Timoleague/Clonakilty. Cross
causeway.

8 TL at TJ, SP Clonakilty/Courtmacsherry.
24km (15 miles)

9 TL, SP Courtmacsherry/Barryroe. Pass
Abbey on RHS.

10 TL, SP Courtmacsherry/Broadstrand.
Cross bridge. Enter Courtmacsherry.

11 TL at XR, SP Broadstrand/Lislee/
Butlerstown. ***32km (20 miles)***

12 TL, SP Butlerstown, for hard climb.

13 TR at XR, SP Butlerstown.

14 TL at TJ (effectively SO), no SP.

36km (22.5 miles)

15 TL (almost back on yourself), no SP. Estuary on LHS. *41.5km (26 miles)*

16 TL, SP Clonakilty.

17 TL at TJ, SP Clonakilty.

53km (33 miles)

18 SO at roundabout along main street, SP Town Centre. Just after statue:

19 TR along McCurtain Hill, no SP (56km/ 35 miles). Continue, passing stone circle on LHS after approximately 2.5km (1.5 miles).

20 SO at XR, no SP (sculpture of Model T Ford on LHS and two pubs on RHS).

62.5km (39 miles)

21 SO at XR, no SP (73km/45.5 miles). Pass Crossmahon Bar on RHS.

22 Bear R opposite Ash Tree pub.

23 TR at TJ along N71, no SP.

24 TL as N71 bears R, no SP (Dew Drop Inn on RHS).

25 TR at TJ opposite Castle Bar, no SP. Pass church on RHS. Continue along South Main Street. At foot of street, TL at XR along St Finbar Place, no SP. Then TR, SP Cork/Inishannon and finish the ride.

77km (48 miles)

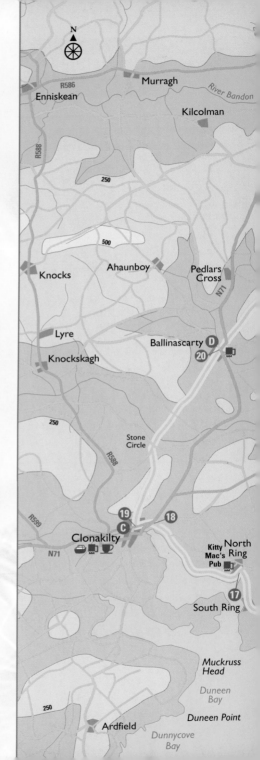

Timoleague

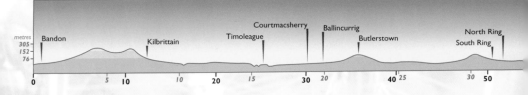

Places of interest along the route

A Bandon

Famous as a Protestant settlement, Bandon for many years excluded the majority Catholic population. The town was established by the Great Earl of Cork, Richard Boyle, who acquired vast estates in Munster having left England virtually penniless. Much of the local history is depicted in the West Cork Heritage Centre which has a recreated bar and shop. Open April to October, Monday–Saturday 1000–1800, Sunday 1400–1800. Charge.

B Timoleague

Attracting a wide variety of migratory birds, Timoleague was once a busy port at the head of Courtmacsherry Bay. The village is dominated by the **Franciscan Abbey** which was founded in 1312 and dedicated to St Mologa. The Franciscan friars who lived here dedicated themselves to strict rules of poverty, which is reflected in the architectural details. In 1642 the English vandalized the abbey, breaking all the stained glass and leaving the ruins seen today. Free access at all reasonable times. The mild climate of this area is demonstrated by the palm trees and rare plant species in **Timoleague Castle Gardens**. The gardens were started by Colonel R Travers in 1820 and have been in the same family ever since. Open June to August, Monday–Saturday 1100–1730, Sunday 1400–1700. Charge.

C Clonakilty

Clonakilty is an attractive town of traditional shop fronts and hand painted signs, many by local crafts people using Irish Gaelic. In the last century, over 100,000 people worked in the linen industry and some of this history is present in the **West Cork Regional Museum**. Open May to October, Monday–Saturday 1030–1730, Sunday 1430–1730. Charge. Much of west Cork's architecture is presented in miniature at the **Model Village**. Also reconstructed 1940s railway station. There are several good beaches within easy reach of Clonakilty. Telephone the Tourist Office on (023) 33226 or visit www.clonakilty.ie for more information on the town and the surrounding area.

D Ballinascarty

Henry Ford's family came from Ballinascarty. To celebrate this, a beautifully shiny Model T Ford sculpture is present by the roadside. What Henry would have thought is debatable as it is not black.

Food and drink

Lots of choice for refreshment in Bandon and Clonakilty. Kilbrittain and Timoleague have shops and pubs. Various shops and pubs are passed en route.

Clonakilty Ballinascarty Bandon Oldchapel

feet
1000
500
250

35   60   40   70   45

miles
kilometres

GLENGARRIFF AND THE BEARA PENINSULA

Route information

Distance   91km (56.5 miles)

Grade   Strenuous

Terrain   Tarmac roads throughout. However, the first section of the route as far as Adrigole is quite pitted and there are numerous short but steep ascents and descents. After this, there are two mountain passes to tackle, separated by a stretch of coastline.

Time to allow   6–10 hours.

Getting there by car   Glengarriff is on the N71. There is on-street parking.

Getting there by train   There is no practical railway access to this route.

From the village of Glengarriff, the route heads west with intermittent views of Bantry Bay. Turning inland, the route offers beautiful, far reaching views as it skirts the Caha Mountains, following the Beara Cycleway. On to cross the mountains via the splendid Healy Pass, before returning along the coast and the north edge of the Beara Peninsula to Kenmare. The final section of the route leads back over the Caha Mountains.

Places of interest along the route

A Glengarriff

Lying in a sheltered area of Bantry Bay, Glengarriff has long been a tourist village. It was the terminal stop in the Prince of Wales route, when a boat to Cork was followed by train to Bantry, culminating in a boat trip to Gengarriff. Today the village contains mostly gift shops and hotels. Contact the Tourist Office on (027) 63084.

B Healy Pass

Cutting through the Caha Mountains, the Healy Pass rises 334m above sea level and was named after Tim Healy, the first governor-general of the Irish Free State. It is here that Cork and Kerry meet – if a Kerry woman married a man from Cork and subsequently produced no children, the custom was for her coffin to be taken to the top and pushed back into Kerry, sending her bad luck with her.

C Dereen Gardens

Planted by the 5th Lord of Lansdowne at the end of the 19th century, the gardens are full of native and exotic plants, including giant conifers from America and tree ferns from New Zealand. Café. Open all year, daily 1000–1800. Charge.

West of Glengarriff

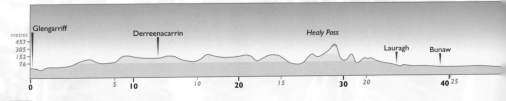

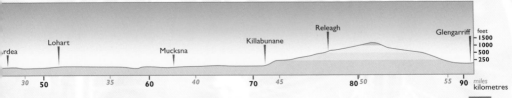

rdea   Lohart   Mucksna   Killabunane   Releagh   Glengarriff   feet
                                                                      1500
                                                                      1000
                                                                      500
                                                                      250

30 50   35   60   40   70 45   80 50   55 90 miles
                                                                      kilometres

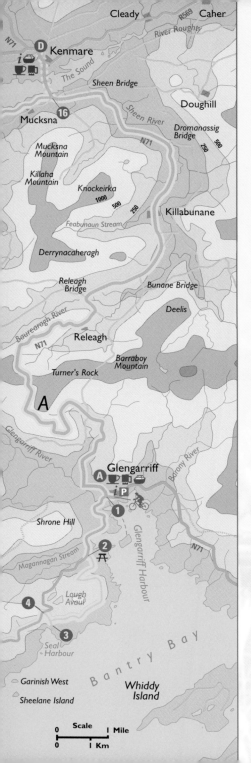

D Kenmare

With its numerous painted frontages, Kenmare is an attractive town boasting a wide variety of places to eat. The **Kenmare Heritage Centre** recounts the history of Kenmare and tells the story of the Nun of Kenmare who advocated women's rights and started the Poor Clare Convent in which women were provided work as needlepoint lacemakers. Charge. Telephone (064) 41491. A short distance out of town is southwest Ireland's largest stone circle – the **Druid Circle** consists of 15 stones and has a central boulder dolmen. Contact the Tourist Office on (064) 41244 for more information.

Route description

Start from the Tourist Office opposite park. Head into centre of Glengarriff.

1   TL, SP Healy Pass/Adrigole/Castletown Bere/Ring of Beara

2   TL along narrow lane, no SP (next to walled single picnic table and sea inlet). Bear acute R at XR and climb. NB: Numerous short, steep ascents and descents make this a hard section. If wish to avoid it, continue SO along R572 to direction 4.

3   TR at TJ, no SP, for steep climb.

9.5km (6 miles)

4   TL at TJ, brown bicycle SP.

5   TR along undulating road, brown bicycle SP. Lovely views.

6   TR, brown bicycle SP/Beara Peninsula SP, for a hard climb.   *16km (10 miles)*

7   TL at TJ, yellow walker SP. Descend and cross bridge.

8 TR (effectively SO), SP Massmount (church). Pass church on LHS.

9 TR at XR, brown bicycle SP.

10 TL at TJ, brown bicycle SP.
23km (14.5 miles)

11 To visit Adrigole, TL.

Otherwise, TR at TJ, SP Cycling via the Healy Pass.

12 TL at TJ, SP Castletown Bere/Ardgroom/ Glanmore Lake. **_37km (23 miles)_**

13 TR, SP Coast Road/Kenmare/ Kilmackillogue Pier.

14 TL at XR, SP Tuosist (48km/30 miles). Make short climb to SO at XR, no SP (telephone box on LHS).

15 TL at TJ (effectively SO), no SP.

16 To visit Kenmare, TL.

Otherwise, TR at TJ, SP Glengarriff/Bantry (65km/40.5 miles). Return to Glengarriff to finish the ride. **_91km (56.5 miles)_**

Food and drink

Glengarriff has shops, pubs and two cafés, one in the centre of town and the other in a disused church on the east side of town. There is a shop and an excellent café by the sea in Adrigole (detour required) and plenty of choice in Kenmare. Several other opportunities for refreshment are passed en route.

Teddy O'Sullivan, Bunaw
Pub opposite the quay serving tea, coffee and sandwiches.

Kenmare

TRALEE AND DINGLE

Route information

Distance 99km (61.5 miles)

Grade Strenuous

Terrain Two long, steep passes – the first is quiet, the second much busier.

Time to allow 6–10 hours.

Getting there by car Tralee is a large town on the N21, just north of the Dingle peninsula. There are several car parks in the town.

Getting there by train There is a railway station at Tralee. For travel information telephone (1850) 366222 or visit www.irishrail.ie

Starting from Tralee, the route uses the two quieter ways of entering and leaving the Dingle Peninsula. Initially there is a steep climb, between Knockmichael Mountain on the right and Knockawaddra on the left, rewarded by far reaching views in both directions. The route then follows the R561 onto the peninsula, with views across Castlemaine Harbour and then Dingle Bay. A stop at Inch is recommended. To avoid the busy N86, the route follows a section of the Dingle Way – this is strenuous cycling and you may prefer to cycle along the N86 instead. The route returns to Tralee over the famous Connor Pass, which although strenuous yields fabulous views and is one of the nicest roads in Ireland.

Places of interest along the route

A Tralee

Sited on the River Lee, Tralee is the capital of Kerry and was founded in 1216. See Route 10 for more information.

B Inch

The lovely 6.5km (4 mile) sand spit at Inch used to be a place of ill repute. In bad visibility wreckers used lanterns to lure ships onto the beach in order to loot them. Today the mudflats and the shallow water provide a haven for many species of sea and wading birds. Diving birds such as shags and gannets search for fish whilst ringed plovers and turnstones can be seen searching for insects on the foreshore. Even though this a popular spot, it is possible to escape the crowds by walking a short distance.

C Freshwater Experience, near Dingle

Set against a mountain backdrop the Freshwater Experience is a combination of three attractions. As a wildlife/wildfowl park there are over 20 different species including otter, boar and rare geese. An archaeological walk takes visitors past wedge tombs, an ogham stone and a crannog (lake dwelling). Finally there is a large fishing lake where visitors can catch a trout for dinner. Coffee shop. Open all year, daily. Charge. Telephone (066) 9151042; www.freshwaterexperience.com

D Dingle

Dingle is an attractive town with much more to offer. See Route 18 for more information.

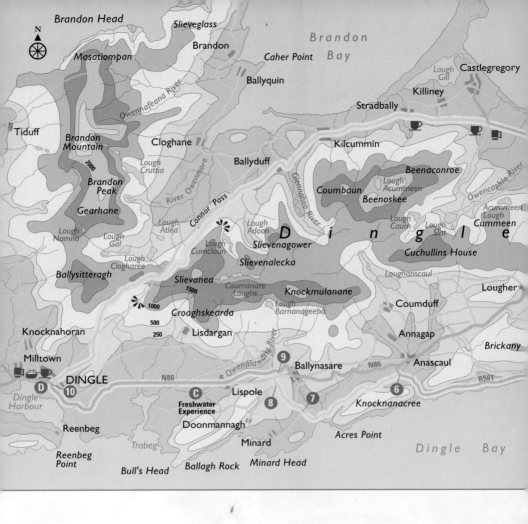

N

Brandon Head
Slieveglass
Brandon
Caher Point
Brandon Bay
Lough Gill
Castlegregory
Masatiompan
Ballyquin
Killiney
Stradbally
Tiduff
Brandon Mountain
Cloghane
Kilcummin
2000
Ballyduff
Beenaconroe
Brandon Peak
Lough Cruttia
River Owenmore
Coumbaun
Lough Acummeen
Gearhane
Connor Pass
Lough Atléa
Lough Adoon
Beenoskee
Lough Caum
Lough Slat
Acummeen Lough
Cummeen
Lough Namna
Lough Gal
D i n g l e
Slievenagower
Cuchullins House
Ballysitteragh
Lough Clogharee
Lough Cumclaun
Slievenalecka
Loughanscaul
Lougher
Slievanea
1500
Coumanare Loughs
Knockmulanane
Coumduff
1000
Croaghskearda
Lough Barnanageeha
Annagap
Brickany
Knocknahoran
500
250
Lisdargan
Owenálanánig River
9
Anascaul
Milltown
N86
Ballynasare
N86
R561
DINGLE
10
C
Freshwater Experience
Lispole
8
7
6
Knocknanacree
Dingle Harbour
D
Doonmannagh
Reenbeg
Minard
Acres Point
Dingle Bay
Trabeg
Reenbeg Point
Bull's Head
Ballagh Rock
Minard Head

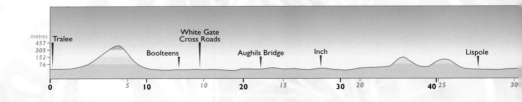

metres
457
305
152
76

Tralee

White Gate Cross Roads

Boolteens

Aughils Bridge

Inch

Lispole

0   5   10   15   20   25   30
         10   20   30   40

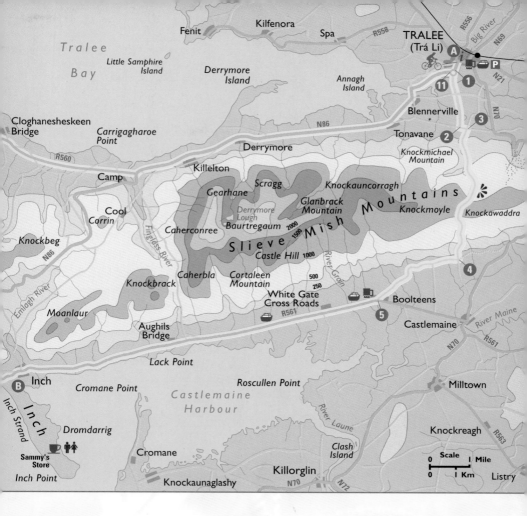

Tralee
Bay

Fenit

Kilfenora

Spa

R558

TRALEE
(Trá Li)

R556

Big River

N69

Little Samphire
Island

Derrymore
Island

Annagh
Island

Blennerville

Tonavane

N70

Cloghanesheskeen
Bridge

Carrigagharoe
Point

N86

Knockmichael
Mountain

R560

Derrymore

Camp

Killelton

Knockauncorragh

Gearhane

Scragg

Glanbrack
Mountain

Knockmoyle

Mountains

Cool
Corrin

Derrymore
Lough

Baurtregaum

2000

Slieve

Mish

Knockawaddra

Knockbeg

N86

Caherconree

1500

Castle Hill

1000

River Gain

Caherbla

Cortaleen
Mountain

500

250

Knockbrack

Emlagh River

Moanlaur

Aughils
Bridge

White Gate
Cross Roads

R561

Booleens

Castlemaine

River Maine

N70

R561

Lack Point

Roscullen Point

River Laune

Milltown

Inch

Cromane Point

Castlemaine
Harbour

Knockreagh

R563

Inch Strand

Inch

Dromdarrig

Clash
Island

Sammy's
Store

Cromane

Killorglin

Listry

Inch Point

Knockaunaglashy

N70

N72

Scale		
0		1 Mile
0	1 Km	

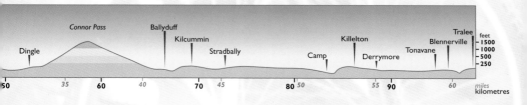

Dingle

Connor Pass

Ballyduff

Kilcummin

Stradbally

Camp

Killelton

Derrymore

Tonavane

Blennerville

Tralee

feet
1500
1000
500
250

50   35   60   40   70   45   80 50   55   90   60

miles
kilometres

Route description

Start by the entrance to the Tourist Office. Head L (town park in front of you). Continue SO, following SP Get in Lane/Dingle/The West.

1 SO at roundabout, SP Steam Train. Pass entrance to Aqua Dome on LHS.

2 TL, SP Scotia's Grave/Castlemaine.

3 TR at XR, no SP, for hard climb (3km/ 2 miles). Admire view and descend.

4 TR at XR, no SP (other direction is a track). **9.5km (6 miles)**

5 TR at TJ, no SP (14.5km/9 miles). Eventually pass Inch Strand on LHS.

6 TL (sharply), no SP (37.5km/23.5 miles). Pass yellow walker SP on LHS. Just after beach:

7 RHF, no SP. **41.5km (26 miles)**

8 TR at TJ, no SP. Pass farm on LHS.

9 TL at XR, no SP (48km/30 miles). Continue into Dingle.

10 TR at roundabout, SP Connor Pass (56km/35 miles). Continue into Dingle, over Connor Pass and into Tralee.

11 TL at roundabout, SP Centre. SO at traffic lights. TR, SP Dingle/Killarney. Walk up one-way street (Ivy Terrace) to finish the ride by the Tourist Office. **99km (61.5miles)**

Food and drink

Plenty of choice in Tralee and Dingle. Various shops, pubs and cafés are passed along the route.

Dingle Bay

A GRAND RANDONNÉE – THE RING OF KERRY

Route information

Distance 130km (81 miles)

Grade Strenuous

Terrain There is a lot of climbing involved in this route. Some of the roads used can be busy.

Time to allow 1–2 days.

Getting there by car Kenmare is on the N71. There is plenty of on-street parking.

Getting there by train There is no practical railway access to this route.

An alternative Ring of Kerry – this route takes in the prettier southern half of Kerry and follows and inland route, full of views and mountains. From Kenmare the route heads south west along the shores of the River Kenmare as far as Waterville. Here the route turns inland into Glencar before heading back to Kenmare. Tourist buses are requested to travel in an anticlockwise direction around the ring and, therefore, should not be too much of a problem. For more information on any of the places mentioned and for details of accommodation en route, contact Kenmare Tourist Office on (064) 41244.

Places of interest along the route

Ⓐ Kenmare

With its numerous painted frontages, Kenmare is an attractive town boasting a wide variety of places to eat. See Route 22 for more information.

Ⓑ Sneem

The picture postcard village of Sneem is worth a visit. In the centre of the village is a small sculpture park featuring, amongst others, a white marble panda from China, a statue of Christ from Singapore and an abstract pyramid. There is a small museum containing exhibits of local interest. Open summer, daily 1000–1300 and 1400–1730. Charge. Visit www.sneem.com for more information.

Ⓒ Staige Fort, near Waterville

Built around 2000 years ago, Staige Fort is one of Ireland's finest dry-stone buildings. The walls are 4m (13 feet) thick in places, and 5.5m (18 feet) high. Its purpose is not known. The building may have been a place of refuge, a fort or even a nobleman's house. The building itself is 4km (2.5 miles) inland from the road, there is an exhibition centre at the roadside that describes the fort through models and sound. Refreshments available. Charge.

Ⓓ Waterville

Overlooking Ballinskelligs Bay, this town is stretched along the seafront. See Route 20 for more information.

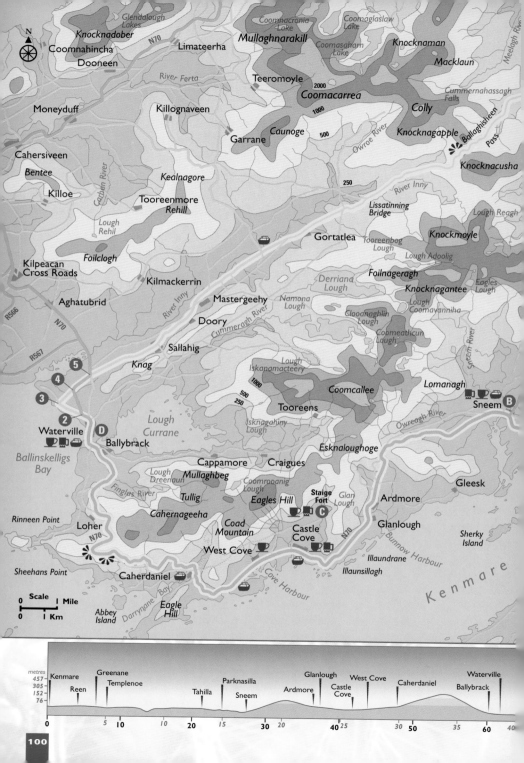

N

Glendalough Lakes
Knocknadober
Coomnahincha
Dooneen
Limateerha
Mullaghnarakill
Coomacronia Lake
Coomaglaslaw Lake
Coomasgham Lake
Knocknaman
Macklaun
N70
River Ferta
Teeromoyle
Coomacarrea
2000
1000
500
Colly
Cummernahassagh Falls
Moneyduff
Killognaveen
Garrane
Caunoge
Owroe River
Knocknagapple
Ballaghisheen
Pass
Cahersiveen
Bentee
Kealnagore
250
Knocknacusha
Killoe
Fertagh River
Tooreenmore
Rehill
River Inny
Lissatinning Bridge
Lough Reagh
Lough Rehil
Foilclogh
Gortatlea
Tooreenbog Lough
Lough Adoolig
Knockmoyle
Kilpeacan Cross Roads
Kilmackerrin
Derriana Lough
Foilnageragh
Eagles Lough
R566
Aghatubrid
Mastergeehy
Namona Lough
Knocknagantee
Lough Coomayanniha
N70
River Inny
Doory
Clooanaghlin Lough
Coomeathcun Lough
R567
Sallahig
Cummeragh River
Lough Iskanamacteery
Lomanagh
Sneem River
5
Knag
1000
500
250
Coomcallee
Sneem
B
4
3
Isknagahiny Lough
Tooreens
Owreagh River
2
Waterville
D
Esknaloughoge
Ballybrack
Ballybrack
Lough Currane
Ballinskelligs Bay
Cappamore
Craigues
Lough Dreenaun
Mullaghbeg
Coomroaganig Lough
Gleesk
Finglas River
Tullig
Eagles Hill
Staige Fort
Glan Lough
Ardmore
Rinneen Point
Cahernageeha
Coad Mountain
Castle Cove
Glanlough
Loher
N70
West Cove
Sherky Island
Illaundrane
Sheehans Point
Bunnow Harbour
Caherdaniel
Illaunsillagh
Abbey Island
Eagle Hill
Darrynane Bay
Cove Harbour
Kenmare

Scale
0   1 Mile
0   1 Km

Elevation profile:

metres
457
305
152
76

Kenmare
Reen
Greenane
Templenoe
Tahilla
Parknasilla
Sneem
Glanlough
Ardmore
Castle Cove
West Cove
Caherdaniel
Ballybrack
Waterville

0   5   10   10   20   15   30   20   40   25   30   50   35   40

Macgillycuddy's Reeks

Coomloughra Lough
Carrauntoohil
Curraghmore
Drishana

E Glencar
Lough Acoose
Lough Curraghmore
Brassel Mountain

Maghanlawaun

1000
500
250

Cromaglan Mountain

Upper Lake

Gearhameen River

River Caragh

Owenroe River

Knockaunanattin
Ballaghbeama Gap

Knocknabreeda

Cummeenduff Lough

Looscaunagh Lough

Owenreagh River

Foardal

Cloon Lough

Knockavulloge
Mullaghanattin

The Pocket

Faher Mountain

Tooreennahone

Lough Brin
1500
1000
Lough Brin

Moll's Gap
9

Eirk Lough

Derrygarriff

Peakeen Mountain

Cappamore

Gowlane

Knocklomena
Fadda Lough
Boughil

Keabduff River
R568

Eskine
Gearha

Derrenfinlehid
Sleivaduff

Letter South

Finnihy River
River Reen

Gortamullin

N71

1
R569

Bogare

8

Knockanaskill

Reen
N70

Knocknafreaghane
Knocknagullion
Letterfinish

Templenoe

Greenane

A
Kenmare

Gearha
R568
N70
500
250

Mucksna
Mucksna Mountain

N71

Knockanamadane

Killaha Mountain

R571
Lohart

Dronoughty River

Dromoughty Lake

Derrynacaheragh

Rossmore Island

Tahilla
Ormonds Island

Congar Harbour

Parknasilla

Ardea

Cloonee Loughs

Inchiquin Lough

Cummer Lough

Knocknagorraveela

Rossdohan Island

Knockagarrane
Knockreagh
1500

Lough Cummeenadillure

Killane Mountain

Turner's Rock

River

R573
Bunaw
Knockanougansh
1000
500

Glanrasna River

Caha

Caha Mountains

N71

Glengarriff River

Ardgroom Harbour

Kilmakilloge Harbour

Coolownig
R571

Lauragh
R574
Knockastumpa

Crosterry Mountain

Barley Lake

Glengarriff

Sallahig
Doory
Mastergeehy
Ballaghisheen Pass
Gearha
Derrenfinlehid
Cappamore
Kenmare

feet
1500
1000
500
250

70   45   80 50   55   90   60   100   65   110 70   120 75   80   miles
kilometres

White Cove

E Glencar

Centred in the middle of Ireland's highest peaks, the area around Glencar is extremely attractive and attracts walkers and climbers who come to enjoy the Macgillycuddy's Reeks to the east and the mountains around Knocknagappie to the west. The area is a designated Area of National Heritage and contains Carrauntoohill, which at 1039m (3409 feet) is Ireland's highest mountain.

Route description

Start from Fair Green, which is the central triangular park in Kenmare. Head out of town with park and telephone on RHS, bars and cafés on LHS.

1 TL, SP Sneem/Caherdaniel. Follow this road through Sneem into Waterville.

2 TL, crown SP (62km/38.5 miles). Follow road along coast.

3 TR, crown SP.

4 TL at TJ onto centrally lined road, crown SP.

5 SO at XR, SP Glencar/Ballaghisheen/Killeenleagh. Continue along this road into Glencar, following SP Ballaghisheen/Glencar.

6 TR at TJ, SP Ballaghbeama Gap/Parknasilla. **93km (58 miles)**

7 Bear R, SP Kenmare/Sneem.

8 TL at TJ, SP Moll's Gap/Killarney. **110km (68.5 miles)**

9 TR at TJ, SP Kenmare. Continue into Kenmare to finish the ride. **130km (81 miles)**

Food and drink

Plenty of choice in Kenmare, with lots of cafés. Sneem, Castle Cove and Waterville have pubs, shops and cafés. Various shops and cafés are passed along the route.

A GRANDE RANDONNÉE – MIZEN HEAD AND SHEEP'S HEAD PENINSULAS

Route information

Distance 131km (82 miles)

Grade Moderate

Terrain Mixed terrain from sections of flat road to climbs.

Time to allow 1–2 days.

Getting there by car Bantry is on the N71. There is plenty of on-street parking.

Getting there by train There is no practical railway access to this route.

A grande randonnée around south west Cork taking in Bantry and the Sheep's Head Peninsula. From Bantry, the route heads along the N71 to Ballydehob. From there back lanes are followed as far as Schull. On through Toormore to climb a small pass onto the northern coast, where there are lovely views across Dunmanus Bay. The route picks up the R591 into Durrus, from where it loops around the attractive Sheep's Head Peninsula and returns to Bantry. For more information on the area and overnight accommodation, contact Bantry Tourist Office on (027) 51796.

Places of interest along the route

A Bantry

One of the main commercial centres of west Cork, at the head of Bantry Bay. The town square has an attractive, expansive feel with statues and seating with views of the bay. A small **museum** run by the Historical Society illustrates the town's past.

B Bantry House

Still occupied by the descendants of the White family who purchased it in 1739, Bantry House overlooks the bay. It is filled with artefacts collected from between 1820 and 1840 by the second Earl who sent back souvenirs from all over Europe. Located in the grounds is the **1796 French Armada Exhibition Centre**, which tells of the ill-fated French invasion of that year when 43 ships left France to incite the Irish to revolt against the ruling English. However, the seas were on the side of England as gales and storms claimed ten boats and only 6000 men reached Bantry Bay. As a result the invasion was aborted and remains from one of the boats are on display. House, gardens and exhibition centre open March to October, daily 0900–1800. Tearoom and craft shop. Charge. Telephone (027) 50047.

C Schull

As the largest village on the Mizen peninsula, Schull is centred around its harbour. Several sailing regattas are held throughout the year,

View to Sheep's Head Peninsula across Dunmanus Bay

Dunmanus Bay

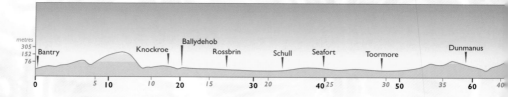

including the annual Calves Week just after Cowes Week on the Isle of Wight, England. The ruins of **St Mary's Church** date from the 16th century and the cemetery contains a famine burial area – between 1841 to 1851 the local population fell from 17314 to 11000. Southern Ireland's only **Planetarium** is sited in the grounds of the local community college. Open March to May, Sunday afternoons only; June, Sunday, Wednesday and Friday, 1500–1700; July and August, Sunday–Thursday 1400–1700 and 1900–2100. Charge.

Ⓓ Sheep's Head Peninsula

Possibly the least visited peninsula, with only a few small settlements. There is a distinct absence of castles, beaches and monuments but what visitors gain are seascapes and a degree of tranquility.

Ⓔ Air India Disaster Memorial

Situated on Sheep's Head Peninsula, the memorial commemorates those who lost their lives when an Air India plane crashed into the sea 192km (120 miles) off the coast of Cork. The memorial is a sundial in a small garden. The names of those who died are inscribed on the surrounding wall and there are extensive views across Dunmanus Bay.

Route description

Start from the Tourist Office. Cycle around large roundabout, passing statue to Theobald Wolfe Tone on RHS. Follow road SO, SP Cork N71 (written on road)/Whiddy Island/Sheep's Head.

1 TR at TJ, SP Ballydehob/Schull/Goleen/Crookhaven (16km/10 miles). Cross bridge. Just after telephone on box LHS and as road bears right:

2 TL, SP The Old Granary B&B. Pass school on LHS.

3 TL at XR, no SP (20km/12.5 miles). Follow telegraph lines on LHS.

4 RHF. Climb briefly.

5 TR at TJ, no SP. Descend to cove. Castle on LHS.

6 TL, no SP. Head towards boat yard for 20m:

7 TR at TJ, no SP, for 50m. Then TL, no SP, and follow lane as it bears L then R to pass to L of boatyard.

8 TL, no SP. Descend.

9 TL at TJ, no SP but house track opposite (23km/14.5 miles). Descend to quay.

10 TL at TJ (acutely), no SP.

11 TL at TJ, no SP. Enter Schull.

12 TL, SP Colla/Hospital. Pass hospital on LHS. Continue along coast.

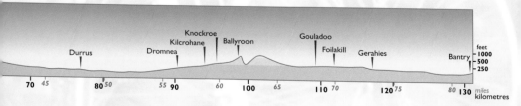

13 TL at TJ, SP Goleen.   *33.5km (21 miles)*

14 TR at TJ, no SP. Pass between two small buildings.

15 SO at XR, no SP – do NOT follow SP Goleen.

16 SO at XR, no SP.

17 SO at XR, no SP.

18 TL at TJ along centrally lined road, no SP.   *38.5km (24 miles)*

19 TR, no SP (junction at point where road bears R). Pass stone wall and bungalow on RHS.

20 TR at TJ, no SP (49km/30.5 miles). Pass under telegraph lines.

21 TL at TJ, SP Durrus/Bantry (54.5km/ 34 miles). Enter Durrus.

22 TL, SP Kilcrohane/Ahakista (69km/ 43 miles). Pass church on RHS. Continue, passing Air India disaster memorial on LHS.

23 TL at TJ, SP Kilcrochane (78.5km/ 49 miles). Pass through Cochrain (Gaelic for Kilcrochane).

24 TR, SP Sheeps Head Cycle Route (house on LHS with bell and anchor on wall), road climbs.   *90km (56 miles)*

25 Follow road SO, ignoring TR turn that appears to be more major and climbs.   *105.5km (65.5 miles)*

26 TL, SP Sheeps Head Cycle Route (126.5km/78.5 miles). Descend steeply.

27 TL at XR, no SP, onto more major road. Return to Tourist Office to finish the ride.   *131km (82 miles)*

Food and drink

Bantry, Ballydehob, Schull, Durrus and Kilcrochane all have shops and pubs.

CTC
(Cyclists' Touring Club)

CTC is the UK's national cycling organisation. With seventy thousand members and affiliates, the club works for all twenty-two million cyclists in England, Wales, Scotland and Northern Ireland. CTC successfully lobbies on behalf of all cyclists and helped the government create its National Cycling Strategy. CTC also campaigns for improved countryside access, better cycling facilities on roads and at the workplace, and more space for bikes on public transport.

CTC provides essential services and invaluable advice for novice and experienced cyclists of all ages and abilities. It has 64 District Associations with 204 local groups plus hundreds of local campaigners in its Right to Ride network. New members and volunteers are always welcomed!

Cyclecover Insurance Services

CTC membership includes free third party insurance and legal aid. CTC also offers several cycling-specific insurance policies. Cyclecover Rescue is a unique twenty-four hour rescue scheme for cyclists stranded by breakdown (excluding punctures), accident, vandalism or theft. CTC offers annual travel insurance and single trip cover. Mountain biking, touring, repatriation of bike, luggage and accessory cover are all included. Comprehensive cycle insurance is offered to members and non-members alike, at very competitive premiums.

CycleSafe

Local authorities are being urged to sign up to four CycleSafe objectives, the aims of which are to improve safety for cyclists. That means reducing risks on roads, consideration for cyclists in new road layouts, adequate investment in cycling facilities and in cycling promotion. CTC has offered all authorities advice on engineering measures, education and examples of successful schemes elsewhere. In York, Britain's most cycling-friendly city, the implementation of a comfortable cycling environment has increased cycling by sixteen per cent and led to a ten per cent drop in cycling casualties in the last 20 years.

Technical and Touring Advice

CTC offers advice on buying a bike and other cycling equipment, maintenance and repair. CTC's events department has information on hundreds of routes both in the UK and abroad and experienced leaders run holidays to scores of destinations throughout the world. These tours are suitable for all cyclists ranging from families with young children to experienced distance riders.

CTC Magazine

Cycle Touring and Campaigning is CTC's bi-monthly magazine which is free to members. Articles cover campaign news, tours, technical advice, event reports and equipment tests.

CTC Help Desk

Staff on the Help Desk answer queries on all things cycling, from contacts at your local group to the best route across the continent. The Help Desk can advise on travelling by train or bus with your bike, bike security and parking facilities in public places and on how to make the workplace more friendly to cyclists.

CTC Membership

Membership costs from just £10 per year. Whether you are a roadster, prefer the quiet of canal paths and the countryside, commute by bike or just enjoy a day out with the children, CTC is the essential accessory for you!

For more information contact the CTC Help Desk:
CTC, 69 Meadrow, Godalming, Surrey GU7 3HS
Telephone 0870 873 0060
Email cycling@ctc.org.uk
Website www.ctc.org.uk

Cyclecover Travel Insurance
For a quote or instant cover:
Telephone 0870 873 0068
Visit www.cyclecover.co.uk

Cyclecover Rescue
Telephone free on 0800 212810.

Cyclecover Cycle Insurance
Telephone free on 0800 169 5798.

CycleSafe
Visit www.cyclesafe.org.uk